Peacock

Animal
Series editor: Jonathan Burt

Already published

Crow
Boria Sax

Ant
Charlotte Sleigh

Tortoise
Peter Young

Cockroach
Marion Copeland

Dog
Susan McHugh

Oyster
Rebecca Stott

Bear
Robert E. Bieder

Rat
Jonathan Burt

Snake
Drake Stutesman

Whale
Joe Roman

Falcon
Helen Macdonald

Bee
Clare Preston

Tiger
Susie Green

Parrot
Paul Carter

Forthcoming

Cat
Katherine M. Rogers

Fly
Steven Connor

Fox
Martin Wallen

Salmon
Peter Coates

Hare
Simon Carnell

Moose
Kevin Jackson

Crocodile
Richard Freeman

Spider
Katja and Sergiusz Michalski

Duck
Victoria de Rijke

Cow
Hannah Velten

Peacock

Christine E. Jackson

REAKTION BOOKS

Published by
REAKTION BOOKS LTD
33 Great Sutton Street
London EC1V 0DX, UK
www.reaktionbooks.co.uk

First published 2006
Copyright © Christine E. Jackson 2006

Printed and bound in Singapore by CS Graphics

British Library Cataloguing in Publication Data
Jackson, Christine E. (Christine Elisabeth), 1936–
    Peacock. – (Animal)
    1. Peafowl
    I. Title
    598.6'258

ISBN-13: 9781861892935
ISBN-10: 1861892934

Contents

Introduction

Across the world, the blue or Indian peacock is recognized and regarded as a most glamorous bird. Remarkably, it is not generally known that there is an even more splendid green peacock and also a much smaller, dumpier, African peacock that does not have the spectacular train.

The blue Indian and green peacocks are two of the most beautiful birds in the world. The blue peacock was so much admired that it was taken from its native haunts in India and Sri Lanka, thousands of years ago, and gradually distributed around the western world. We do not know when it was first introduced into Britain, but it was a long time ago. That such an exotic bird became so familiar as an inhabitant of our gardens and barnyards is a tribute to its hardiness and adaptability as much as to its beauty.

Apart from the wonderful, brilliant plumage and extraordinary performance in raising its long train in a remarkable display, this is a bird of distinctive character. We think of the peacock as a thoroughly masculine bird, proud, showing off, flamboyant and aggressive. We accuse him of strutting proudly, even referring to him when displaying as being 'in his pride'. His propensity to show off has recently been evoked to describe the manner in which human youths behave. It has been found that separating boys from girls into different classes at school

A male blue peacock displaying.

7

has improved the academic results of both. Educationalists put this down to removing the 'peacock effect'.

The most impressive characteristic of the blue and green peacocks is their ability to lift their train feathers into a huge arc, 1.8–2.1 metres wide, and walk round with this display, shimmering and rattling the feathers. It is a breathtaking display

for the human viewer, although the peahen appears to be indifferent. She behaves as though she has seen it many times before, day after day, week after week, every springtime – as indeed she has. Her only apparent response is to peck studiously at minute particles of food on the ground. This studied indifference has intrigued scientific observers, including Charles Darwin. In the 1990s scientists made careful observations of females and their choice of mates and proved that the apparently disinterested and otherwise engaged females are actually far more observant than would appear. They choose for mates, and lay more eggs for, males with the largest trains. It is three years before a peacock's train attains its full length, largest eyespots (ocelli) and most intense colour. The peahen's discerning eye carefully selects the most glamorous and mature male, rejecting younger, less splendid birds.

J. J. Grandville's caricature of a man full of pride, like a peacock. He boasts: 'I'm a millionaire, with five castles, a host of friends.'

An 1860s wood engraving of blue peacocks.

Despite having been part of our bird community for centuries, little has been written about the blue peacock and few facts are generally known about the birds by others than aviculturalists. Only a few books have been devoted entirely to the peacock, although illustrations of the bird appear in the earliest manuscripts. A little more was written about them in general natural histories and in monographs when books on the Galliformes (the avian order containing peacocks as well as their close relatives, the pheasants, partridges, quails and jungle fowl) were first published in the nineteenth century, but it was not until the late twentieth century that a book solely about peacocks was published.

The peacock is recognized as a symbol in the religions of its natural Asian habitats, where it is a vehicle for gods in the Hindu and Buddhist religions. It is also the subject of fairy stories, myths and legends. In the west, one of the most famous legends about the peacock, known to both Greeks and Romans, is how it acquired the eye-spots in its train feathers. The chief god Jupiter and his wife the goddess Juno were responsible for the remarkable ocelli being placed in the peacock's plumage. Jupiter could never resist a beautiful human maiden, and this made Juno extremely angry when she caught him out. One of these unfortunate females was Io, whom Jupiter had to transform quickly into a cow in an attempt to hide her from his wife's anger. Juno demanded the cow be given to her and charged her cowherd, Argus, who had one hundred eyes all over his body and so never slept, with the task of guarding Io. Argus was killed and Juno preserved his hundred eyes by transferring them onto the train feathers of her royal bird, the peacock.

Other stories about the peacock's train, its voice and even its feet abound in the literature of both east and west, but awareness of the presence of the peacock in our midst has

varied in intensity over the centuries. There have been several periods when the peacock has been prominent. It was present in early Christian art in illustrated manuscripts and paintings of biblical scenes such as the *Garden of Eden*, the *Creation* and *Noah's Ark*. In medieval manuscripts the illuminators revelled in the opportunity to paint all the bird's intense colours. During the Middle Ages, it was a source of feathers for fletching arrows and for personal adornment of men's helmets and hats, and on heraldic devices. During the seventeenth-century Golden Age of Dutch and Flemish painting, the peacock was frequently present in pictures of both the barnyard and aristocratic gardens. Little was seen of peacocks for the next century, then they became important again for embellishing millinery – this time for women. The excessive use of their feathers for this purpose contributed to the establishment of the Society for the

Argus guarding Io after she has been turned into a cow by Jupiter, in a 1490s fresco by Pinturicchio in the Borgia Apartments in the Vatican, Rome.

After the death of Argus, Juno and her *putti* placed his eyes in the train of her symbolic bird, seen here in a detail from a Renaissance tapestry.

A 16th-century Iznik plate from Turkey, with the pattern that inspired William De Morgan's design (opposite).

Protection of Birds in 1891 and the National Audubon Society of America in 1886. At the end of the nineteenth century and the beginning of the twentieth they were such an integral and iconic part of the Arts and Crafts and Art Nouveau movements' outpouring of metalwork, tiles, glass, ceramics and other artefacts that it was impossible to avoid their image. For the last hundred years, they have again merged into the background, seen only in large gardens where they can roam in a semi-domesticated state.

For thousands of years, these magnificent birds have had a close association with man in diverse ways. Few other bird species have had such a varied and extensive history, holding a

prominent place in the culture, art and religion of eastern and western nations. It has been a survivor, a truly remarkable bird reputed to have an angel's feathers, the voice of the devil and the feet of a thief.

1 Natural History

The earliest history of peacocks cannot be definitively established, mainly because bird skeletons do not lend themselves well to the process of fossilization. The fossil records for the Galliformes, the bird order to which peacocks belong, are incomplete. They show that fowl-like birds were differentiated and well established as a group early in Tertiary times, 26 million years ago. In 2003 there was a report of finding an Ethiopian Pliocene fossil, a link between the living Asian and African peacocks, a large *Pavo* species, morphologically distinct, but closer to the blue and green peacocks than to the Congo peacock. It was suggested that the Congo peacock, *Afropavo*, diverged from the *Pavo* around the Middle/Late Miocene (26 to 7 million years ago). Little other evidence has so far been found of the peacock's earliest history.[1]

What we have, and in surprising abundance, is evidence of the movement of the blue peafowl across land and sea from its native India and Sri Lanka to Europe in the centuries BC. There is less information about the movement of the green peafowl of Burma and Indo-China, east and north through China and to Japan, because these birds are far less amenable than the blue species to being moved or kept in captivity. The Congo peacock was not even discovered by a naturalist until 1936, and appears to be confined to the Congo (Zaire) now, but its earlier distribution is unknown.

A watercolour of a displaying blue peacock by Nicolas Robert (1614–1685). A rare portrait of the bird strutting, and a remarkable attempt for the time to capture the effect of 100 to 150 train feathers with their ocelli and longer v-shaped feathers.

Peacocks are close relatives of pheasants, nearly all of which come from Asia. The Congo peacock is the only species of pheasant that is naturally distributed outside Asia. All peacocks have iridescent plumage with impressive displays, small heads, long necks and strong spurred legs (unusually, the females also carry spurs). Like pheasants, they all roost in trees for safety. Another characteristic they have in common with pheasants is their preference for thick, shady undergrowth where they skulk and are difficult to observe. Consequently, the status of the Congo peacock is largely unknown in the wild, and that of the green is only slightly less difficult to ascertain. Studying them in captivity has proved equally hard, because few green peacocks are held in aviaries, and there were only 108 specimens of the Congo peacock in captivity in 1996. There is more information on the behaviour and ecology of the blue peafowl, mainly because it is more adaptable to the presence of human beings.

Blue female
peacock with
week-old chicks
and blue male
peacock.

The widespread distribution of blue peacocks, away from their native homelands of India and Sri Lanka, has made them a familiar sight in many countries. The metallic sheen of their feathers and brilliant colouring of the spectacular train that has been displayed before countless humans, not to mention peahens, is a constant source of wonder and delight.

Birds' feathers are made of cells of keratin, the same substance from which hair and nails, horns and hooves, are composed. The structural arrangement of the keratin, rather than pigments, accounts for the plumage iridescence, which occurs as the change in colour is observed with different viewing angles. Much of the blue peacock's plumage is iridescent, the neck and breast being cobalt blue, the back and rump gold, and the train (upper tail coverts) of several colours.

The back and rump feathers of the cock are a glistening gold, shown off at their best when the bird is displaying as a contrast to the deep blue of the neck. The fulvous or cinnamon-coloured primary wing feathers, which are not iridescent, form a lovely contrast to the greens and golds of the train. The train feathers, formed from the upper tail coverts, are made up of disintegrated metallic barbs, which are coppery-brown/gold and dark green. More than 100 have the ocelli, but some 30 to 40 longer feathers are golden-green and end in a broad, v-shaped fan. Sickle-formed side feathers are again a glittering gold-green and form a fringed outer border to edge the raised train. Some of these have a smaller eye-spot.

Although it may look cumbersome, the train, carried an inch or two off the ground, does not inconvenience the bird either while running through vegetation or beating up into his roost. Peafowl are able to rise rapidly and at a remarkably sharp angle.

The 20 tail feathers supporting the train of a displaying blue peacock.

Once on the wing, the bird flies beautifully and can make the same speed as a pheasant. It frequently perches on a high branch, where it may be conspicuous, but safe. As it prepares to roost, the bird flies onto a lower branch, then works its way higher, branch by branch, until it has reached its top perch.[2]

When the male peacock does not wish to be seen, it can disappear among foliage and become very difficult to spot. Even a muster of fifteen or twenty birds can vanish without trace within seconds. An American naturalist, Gerald Handerson Thayer, wrote a book called *Concealing Coloration in the Animal Kingdom* (1909) with a theory about the manner in which animals are protected when in their natural habitats by the colours of their fur and feathers blending in with the colours of their surroundings. One of the plates in this book showed the peacock camouflaged in the undergrowth.

The peacock caused Charles Darwin a good deal of anxiety. The seemingly inefficient and obviously extravagant train, which would attract the attention of predators, flouted Darwin's rules of natural selection. He even confessed, in a letter to Asa Gray of 3

Abbot H. Thayer's oil painting *Peacock in the Woods*, 1907, demonstrating the difficulty of seeing peacocks in vegetation, was undertaken as part of the thesis of his book *Concealing Coloration in the Animal Kingdom* (1909).

April 1860, that while formulating his theories about evolution, the very 'sight of a feather in a peacock's tail [*sic*], whenever I gaze at it, makes me sick'. His problem was that the train not only made the male more conspicuous to its enemies, but was also thought to hamper its escape from them. Darwin eventually solved the problem with a second theory – of sexual selection. The plumage had evolved over time to give the males an advantage in mating. All the adult males had the magnificent trains, so it was the cocks with the largest eye-spots and most brilliant colours that would be more likely to be favoured by the females.[3]

Since it is the females who choose the bird with whom they will mate, this theory was investigated recently at Whipsnade Zoo in Bedfordshire, by sociobiologist Marion Petrie. She recorded that the blue peahens deliberately chose the males whose train feathers carried the largest eye-spots. She then followed the careers of the chicks sired by different males, and found that the offspring of the most ornamental males not only grew faster but had a better survival rate.[4]

In India, the male birds are in full plumage from June to December, the peahen laying eggs and nesting during July and August, the rainy season. The 1.2-metre-long train is discarded entirely in January. (In captivity in England, the moult occurs from July, when the cocks lose their train, the retrices and the wing feathers. In October/November, new growth begins but the new coverts remain short until there is rapid growth in the spring, with the bird's full splendour restored in April/May.) Both sexes go through this period of swift moulting, long recovery and then rapid regrowth, though the female carries no train. In the period when they have short feathers, the males appear to be 'off colour' and seek seclusion.

The long history of the export of feathers is easily understood when 100 plumes each year could be collected from a single male at the time of the moult. It was a lucrative source of income, for very little trouble, especially where the birds were to be found in large musters.

In countries outside the normal range of the peacocks' distribution, a few wealthy people became familiar with the birds' train feathers long before they saw skins, stuffed specimens or live peacocks. For anyone seeing a single plume with its brilliant eye-spot and glittering barbules for the first time, a feather was a valuable and desirable object to own. Feathers were bought and placed in cabinets of curios, like rare shells and precious stones.

Feathers were worn for personal adornment in head-dresses and in coats by natives of the countries where the birds lived. The cloth was made from a silk warp and the woof of feathers

Peacocks in an old Armenian manuscript.

and it was probably such a coat that was sent by Pope Paul III (1534–49) to the French monarch. In countries far from the birds' natural haunts, the feather trade has supplied plumes for emblems of rank, to decorate hats and helmets, fans and fly-swats, flies for fishermen, fletching for archers' arrows, and, more recently, flower arranging and decorative crafts. An ornithologist first became aware of the existence of the Congo peacock when he saw two hitherto unknown feathers in a native head-dress. Early accounts of the birds' presence in countries outside their normal range might refer only to feathers that had been taken there, long before a live bird had been imported.

The peacock's stout legs have given rise to adverse comments both serious and facetious. Coloured greyish horny-brown with darker claws, they are typical gallinaceous – or barnfowl – legs, which sit oddly with the glamour of the rest of the bird. Not many birds have stories about their feet, but the peacock has been accused of being so ashamed of its large legs and feet that when it catches sight of them it stops displaying and cries aloud in protest at having them imposed on it. Robert Chester in his poem 'Love's Martyr' of 1601 described the effect of its feet on the bird:

The proud sun-bearing Peacock with his feathers
Walks all along, thinking himself a king,
And with his voice prognosticates all weathers,
Although God knows but badly he doth sing;
But when he lookes downe to his base-blacke Feete,
He droopes and is asham'd of things unmeete.

In reality, they are powerful aids when escaping, for all peacocks prefer to run into thickets rather than take flight. They can run at speed, outdistancing a pursuing man over a short distance. The spurs are only 2.5 centimetres long but can be used to slash at another male like fighting-cocks in defence of territory at breeding time. Fights take place with males facing each other, leaping in the air and raking downwards. One fierce contest began some distance from Chester, where two peacocks 'became so excited while fighting, that they flew over the whole city, still fighting, until they alighted on the top of St John's tower'.[5]

The curious gait of the peacock, especially while displaying his train, has led to it being accused of swaggering and strutting. However, the stiff-legged strut and apparent swagger are due merely to the mechanical effort to keep balanced. In a high wind, these movements are correspondingly exaggerated and peacocks are reluctant to display when it is very windy. Shakespeare caught the gait of the peacock when he described it as 'a stride and a stand', likening it to the walk of Ajax in *Troilus and Cressida* (III. iii, 253–4).

The peacock's call, said to resemble *paa-vo*, is described as being harsh, strident, screeching and unpleasant. This is the reaction of people who are close to the bird when it is kept in a semi-domesticated state. Edward Baker, writing about the birds in the Indian forests, said:

> The call of the Peacock is rather a fine cry when heard in the wilds far from any human habitation, though so penetrating and unpleasant when at close quarters in a farmyard . . . They often call on moonlight nights when, except for the drone and hum of insects, the Indian nights are silent, broken by the loud 'phi-ao, phi-ao' of a cock Peafowl, the call being taken up by bird after bird until the last cries died away in the distance.[6]

When disturbed by the bigger forest animals, like elephant, bear or deer, they call with a few loud cries, but if a member of the cat tribe is spotted they will shout as long as it is within sight, often following the cat from one tree to another for a considerable distance.

Blue peacocks live for 20–25 years, breeding from their third year onwards. The female normally lays three to five oval, buff eggs with thick, glossy shells, deeply pitted with small pores. The eggs are said to be very tasty and, where religious strictures do not forbid the eating of the eggs, hundreds are eaten by natives. The nest is a mere scrape on the ground with a few dry sticks and leaves, hidden away under shrubs. The chicks run around as soon as hatched and take a few weeks to become independent. Male chicks take three years before they have a full train.

The birds are at their most spectacular in the breeding season when the polygamous males spend a good deal of time displaying. The train in full breeding plumage projects from 100 to 120 centimetres (sometimes more) beyond the end of the true tail. The 100–150 raised train feathers, supported behind by the

White peacock
male displaying.

20 stiff tail feathers, radiate out to form a huge arc 180 to 210 centimetres in width that is arched forwards towards the female. At the same time, the body is bent, as if bowing. The male then shakes or shimmers the train, which makes a clearly audible rustling sound. The gold of the rump and back feathers forms a superb foil for the iridescent blue of the breast, against the glittering rainbow display feathers. The mounting of the female lasts a few seconds.

Male white peacock from a North Korean postage stamp of 1988.

Peacocks are omnivorous, eating land-shells, insects, worms, small lizards, tiny frogs and snakes. The name of the peacock in Sanskrit is *mayura*, meaning 'killer of snakes'. Mostly, however, they feed on grain and tender juicy shoots of grass and bamboo, flower-buds and petals, especially tree-buds. Perhaps their favourite food is fat termites. They can be destructive of plantations if found there in numbers. They also swallow small pebbles and grit.

Abundant water is necessary, for peacocks are thirsty birds. By forest pools, where they gather together, they are especially vulnerable to attack. Peacocks do not bathe in water, preferring to have dust baths. After a good dust bath, which helps to rid the bird of insects and external parasites, it spends a good deal of time preening its feathers. If the peacock gets his train wet, as he does in the early morning when it becomes drenched with dew, he waits on his roost until the feathers have dried.

The peacock naturally seeks seclusion, except where long experience has taught it that it has nothing to fear, as in Indian temples and villages where it is revered and protected. Its gait is that of a bird that steps warily, while its upright carriage with constant movement of the head is that of a bird alert to danger. Its display is part of its attempt to entice a female to mate, but can also be intimidatory when other males are in the vicinity or danger from other species threatens. Its cry acts as a warning to other creatures of predators in the vicinity, besides establishing territorial claims.

The main enemies of the peacock are the large cats: civet, tiger and leopard, and wild dogs, including the dhole and jackal. When attacked, the peacock will run at speed through scrub and dense vegetation, rather than take flight. If it has to take flight, once on the wing it flies at a fair pace, contrary to many naturalists' and sportsmen's belief. It is most at risk of becoming a victim of surprise attacks while drinking; while the male is displaying with its train erected and it is unable to see behind it; and while roosting if it has not flown sufficiently high up in the tree. The long train can be tugged by tiger claws to dislodge a roosting bird. With the train well over a metre in length, and a tiger able to stretch 3 metres (more, if it jumps), the bird needs to be on a branch at least 5.5 metres from the ground to be entirely safe from a tiger. Young tigers hone their stalking and pouncing skills on peacocks.

Charles R. Knight (1874–1953) considered this oil painting (done at the Bronx Zoo), *A Tiger with Peacock* to be his finest, and kept it in his studio until his death. In the wild, the tiger might have caught the peacock drinking at a similar pool.

Blue peacocks were once found in abundance in many parts of India and Sri Lanka. In 1807 Captain Thomas Williamson wrote of seeing at least 1,200 or 1,500 peacocks within sight of the spot where he stood.[7] His depredations and those of many others, plus the human population expansion, contributed to spoiling this picture of peacock heaven on earth. Today, man is still the peacock's greatest enemy, mainly because in many parts of its natural range deforestation programmes are reducing its habitat. Attempts have been made to extend the range of the blue peacock by programmes to naturalize the bird in different parts of the world. There is now a small feral population in the Andaman Islands, USA, Australia, New Zealand and some Hawai'ian Islands.[8] The bird is being protected in national parks and the Indians, in particular, are making great efforts to conserve both birds and habitats.

In the late twentieth century there was a great increase in the number of aviculturalists (especially in the US) who kept blue peacocks in semi-domestic conditions. In mild winters in southern Britain, they survive with little more than a shelter for the worst weather. In the north, the damp and cold combined can be a problem for them. Vet David Taylor commented that

At Belle Vue, Manchester, in the zoo as October came round, cases of disease and death began to soar. Peacocks hacked away like chain-smokers, tigers heaved their chests with the desperate concentration of asthmatics, and chimps wiped running eyes and nostrils with the backs of hairy hands.[9]

There are three aberrant variations of the blue peacock, white, pied and black-winged. White peacocks are seen in many wild musters, as well as among captive birds. Entirely white

Jakob Bogdani,
*A Pair of Peafowl
in a Park*, c. 1710,
oil on canvas.
A female pure
white, and a male
pied, peafowl in
front of the Earl of
Halifax's Baroque
water garden in
London's Bushy
Park.

birds are not true albinos for they have the normal brown eyes and breed true. The ocelli on the train are palely visible. They are every bit as spectacular and as beautiful as their coloured relations. Some birds exhibit the odd white feather among their normal plumage, giving a pied effect. The bird may have a white peacock in its ancestry, but no one is quite sure why this occurs.

A black-winged
peacock.

A black-winged peacock was first mentioned by John Latham in 1823, appearing as a melanistic mutation living among normal flocks.[10] It is a mutation that has occurred only in captivity, classified as *Pavo cristatus* mut. *nigripennis*. The bird is thought by many to be more beautiful than the common blue peafowl, and the ordinary barred buff and black scapulars (shoulders), and wing-coverts, are replaced by black feathers with lustrous dark blue and green borders and tips. The females and chicks of the black-winged birds are cream-coloured. Hybrids, usually between a green cock and black-shouldered blue hen, were developed in America in the first half of the twentieth century by Mrs Keith Spalding of California, where they are well established, breed true, and are called Spalding's Peafowl.

The first record of the common blue peafowl in what is now the USA was the introduction by Frances Sinclair of birds on the island of Kauai, Hawai'i, in 1860. There are many breeders of both blue and green peacocks in America today.

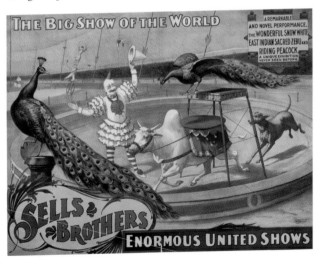

An 1890s Sells Brothers circus poster with 'riding peacock'.

GREEN OR SCALED PEACOCK, *PAVO MUTICUS*, LINNAEUS, 1766

The Javanese green peacock and the blue peacock, with crests on the back of their heads.

The blue peacock ocellus (left) has long disintegrated green-gold barbs; the green peacock ocellus (right) is rounder in shape with bronze-green barbs. Both feathers are around one metre long.

The green peacock differs from the blue peacock and is easily distinguished from it physically by the cock and hen being brighter and greener in colour; in his peculiar facial colouring; the long barbed crest of straight, stiff, narrow feathers; a voice that is not as loud, less frequently heard and of a deeper tone; and longer legs. The effect of the display of *Pavo muticus* is more of a golden-bronze hue.

The crest feathers, shaped like an ear of wheat, are of a metallic blue, shaded with green, the longest of these being nearly 13 cm in length. The entire forehead, crown and anterior part of the occiput are covered with closely set scaly feathers, tipped with brilliant metallic blue, shaded with green. This gave rise to the alternative name of scaled green peacock. The feathers of the neck and breast are tipped with a broad band of bronze green. There is no barring of the lesser wing-coverts, tertiaries or scapulars as in the blue peacock. Green females have a brighter plumage than blue females, looking more like the males but without the train. Their longer legs and more slender stance give them an even prouder appearance.

There are three subspecies of green peacocks, divided according to which area they inhabit, all of them to the east and not overlapping the range of the blue peacock whose natural haunts are in India and Sri Lanka. Green peacocks replace the blue from south-eastern Assam through Burma, Yunnan, Laos and Thailand to the China Sea and southwards to the Malay peninsula and Java, but do not occur either in Borneo or Sumatra.

The most vivid green bird is the Javan green peafowl *Pavo muticus muticus*, Linnaeus, 1766, described above. The Indo-

Joseph Wolf's lithograph of a pair of green peafowl for Daniel Giraud Elliot's *Monograph of the Phasianidae* (1872).

Chinese peafowl *Pavo muticus imperator*, Delacour, is not quite so brilliant a green, and there are a few subtle differences, but describing the colours of peacocks is always a tricky task owing to the constantly changing shades of the iridescent feathers.[11]

The Burmese green peafowl *Pavo muticus spicifer*, Shaw and Nodder, 1804 (Latin *spica*, an ear of corn), differs from the other two *Pavo muticus* species more radically.[12] The plumage is bluer and duller, with the neck and upper breast feathers lacking the rich bronze colouring; also the back is bluer and less golden. The distinctive facial skin colouring is not so strongly blue and yellow.

Allan Octavian Hume (1829–1912), a British civil servant in India, knew both blue and Burmese green peacocks well. He spent months collecting birds in Burma in 1879 and said that the finest Burmese peacock he ever saw was 90 inches (2.3 m) from the tip of its bill to the end of its train. His personal observations of the birds in their natural habitats, when still relatively unmolested, are invaluable. He also stated that the metallic sheen varies in colour in different lights, so the emerald green may predominate, or deep blue, or copper colours.

All the green peacocks are very shy and retire into jungle, shunning the vicinity of villages. They are found in small colonies in isolated patches (not in large musters as the blue peacock), making them more difficult to hunt; it is not often that one is secured with a gun. They are also very keen-sighted and sharp of hearing. When it is necessary to escape, the male trusts to his legs rather than his wings, and can run at an amazing pace, even when in possession of a full train. Green peacocks sleep in the forest but venture out daily to feed in fields if there is cultivation near at hand. Because they need a good supply of water, they live within reach of small hill rivers and streams.

Another British civil servant, with the Indian police, commented:

Cock birds are extremely pugilistic and fierce, and have been quite frequently known to kill each other in their combat and even to kill hens to whom they had taken a dislike. The display of spreading train, drooping wings and strutting walk is similar to that of the Indian Peafowl and, like that of that bird, is used as a means of intimidation as well as of incitement to the hen bird.[13]

Its voice is less frequently heard, not as loud, deeper in tone and more like a mew, mew, mew. It, too, calls to warn of tigers.

During the moult in August, the males drop their long ocellated tail-coverts and assume simpler green-barred ones. The train lengthens again in the following March or April. The moulting time is irregular. The male has a small harem of three to five females, but only the hen incubates, usually during the rains. The males calling at mating time, during the rainy season, gave rise to the belief that the peacock's call predicted the coming of rain. The young hatch at different times from August until January. They all look like miniature females for the first year; the males of the second year are similar to the cock but with shorter train feathers and lacking the ocelli of the third year and mature males.

Keeping green peacocks in captivity is much more difficult than caring for blue peacocks. They are less hardy, need protection from frost and intense cold, and do not like coexisting with other species in aviaries. Because of their aggressive nature, male green peacocks have to be kept separately from others of their own species, as well as from smaller birds of any other species.

The less hardy nature of the green species, coupled with its aggressiveness and the difficulty in capturing the birds alive, explains the lack of success in distributing them outside their

A Congo peacock female from a North Korean postage stamp of 1990.

natural homelands. While most people in the west have seen blue peacocks, few have seen a green one in captivity.

CONGO PEACOCK, *AFROPAVO CONGENSIS*, CHAPIN, 1936

The third peacock caused a sensation in the ornithological world in 1937. For centuries the Congolese were familiar with their *mbulu* bird, ate it and used its feathers for personal ornament, while it remained unknown in Europe and thus undescribed and unnamed for science.

Despite nineteenth-century explorations of the Congo, this bird escaped the notice of the west until an American ornithologist, Dr James P. Chapin, who was an employee of the American Museum of Natural History, New York, went on an expedition to the Congo in 1909–15. While in Avakubi, Chapin met a native who wore the usual touraco feather head-dress, but had added two other very unusual feathers, reddish in colour with broad black bands. These two feathers were from a bird that Chapin had never seen, either in museum collections or alive. He bought the head-dress from the man who told him the two feathers were from the *mbulu* bird. Chapin could not find the *mbulu* bird in the Congo and failed to find a specimen of any bird with these feathers for twenty years. While writing *The Birds of the Belgian Congo* in 1936, he went to the Congo Museum at Tervueren, near Brussels, searched the cabinets and looked round the lumber rooms. In one room, awaiting disposal, were two mounted birds in a bad state of preservation, covered in dust. They were larger than domestic poultry, one blackish, the other red in colour. The reddish bird had black-striped wing feathers that awoke a memory. They were obviously peacocks, but Africa was thought then not to have any peacocks in its avifauna. The pair of birds had been donated to the museum by the Kasai Trading Company, which had had a trading monopoly in the southern Congo State before the First World War.

Several contacts were made with Belgians who had served in the Congo, some of whom it transpired owned a specimen of the bird, or had memories of seeing or eating it (pronouncing it very tasty but the breast needed well larding). Chapin returned to the Congo in 1937, to the jungle along the Ayena River to observe them for himself. He saw them scuttling through the shrubs and heard their hoarse cry.

Chapin returned to America with specimens, and named and described the bird *Afropavo congensis*, being able to give some description of its habits and habitat. Few scientists have seen the bird in Congo/Zaire since that date, and it was not for another twenty years that the first live specimens were taken to America.[14] However, there are dense areas of the Congo still unexplored where Congo peacock groups may live. They are protected now in the Maiko National Park and in the interior of the Kahuzi-Biega National Park.

Unlike the blue and green peacocks, this species is monogamous and less vociferous, calling mostly at night. Both sexes have a vertical crest; the female's is chestnut coloured, that of the male white at the base and black at the tips. The neck and throat are bare. It looks like a primitive form of the blue and green peacocks, with the beautiful back and tail feathers iridescent green and lower neck and breast feathers glossy blue-purple, but it lacks the long train. When displaying, the male faces the female, raises its tail feathers in a fan, which is then curved over to the rear, and gives a low call. The Congo peacock also has a lateral display, similar to those of pheasants. The wing on one side is lowered, on the other side raised, while the fanned tail is tilted to one side. The head is lowered and moved toward the female onlooker. The female can reply with a display of fanned tail and drooped wings.[15]

The species is confined to the rain forests of the east central Congo/Zaire at altitudes of between 365 and 1,500 metres. It has not been naturalized anywhere else and the few birds taken alive to other parts of the world have been kept in captivity with varying success. The birds rarely breed while on show, only if placed in a secluded and sheltered place, with warm temperatures.

The first live birds to leave the Congo were sent to New York Zoo in 1947 by the collector Charles Cordier. The same collector sent further pairs to Antwerp Zoo between 1959 and 1962, and a brood of three young was reared there in 1964.[16] Today, there are 20 zoos worldwide that have Congo peafowl in their collections. Foremost among them, Antwerp Zoo established a Congo Peafowl Trust in 1971. Chester Zoo successfully breeds them.

This species may not be easy to raise in captivity, but with loss of its forest habitat in its native country, combined with snaring by natives and mining activities, it is going to require programmed propagation of birds in order to survive. Prolonged fighting in the Congo civil war has seen the slaughter of many Congo peacocks, some for soldiers' food, and the bird is regarded as facing a high risk of extinction in the wild in the medium-term future. The new Salonga National Park in Zaire, 3.6 million hectares, is in the centre of the species' range, so a degree of protection has now been accorded it.

While naming species, naturalists look for physical features that they can represent in the genus and species names. Eye-spots are obvious distinctive features and ones that instantly remind one of peacocks' ocelli. Consequently, several species of other birds, of butterflies, shells, fish and plants, bear the adjective 'peacock' in their English names, and *pavo, pavonina, pavoninus* in their scientific names. In addition, there are others that have incorporated in their names the characters in the story of the manner in which the peacock acquired its ocelli, Argus and Io (see Introduction).

Other bird species to have peacock incorporated into their names are the closely related Peacock Pheasants, and a Peacock Cuckoo *Dromococcyx pavonina* that acquired its sobriquet from having a rufous crown and crest. The Crowned Crane *Balearica pavonina*, similarly, has a topknot of chestnut-coloured feathers. The Pavonine Quetzal *Pharomachrus pavoninus* has glittering green feathers and a very long tail, occasioning the comparison with a peacock. More often, it is the ocelli, spots of colour surrounded by a ring of another colour, that suggested the name 'peacock' to ornithologists, and the Peacock Pheasants are the outstanding example of this. There are three Bronze-tailed Peacock Pheasants and three Grey Peacock Pheasants, all Asian species.

One of the most famous pictures of a blue peacock in full display was painted by Archibald Thorburn, in watercolour, in 1917. He included a Peacock Butterfly, *Inachio io*, in the foreground, which incorporates the name of the maiden Io, seduced by Jupiter. There is also a spotted Peacock Moth, *Macaria notata*.

The tiny humming-bird, *Polemistra pavoninus* (Peacock Coquette), has elongated green neck feathers with a conspicuous spot near the apex of each feather. Black spots on fishes, shells, flowers and butterflies are commonly associated with peacocks.

Peacock Bass (including *Cichla ocellaris*) are big-game fish in the Amazon and Rio Negro rivers, and elsewhere in Mexico and America. They have a characteristic large black eye-spot encircled by a silver halo on the caudal fin. The Peacock of the Sea, Peacock Fish or Peacock Wrasse, *Crenilabrus (Thalassodroma) pavo*, is a blue-striped Atlantic fish whose juveniles have two large ocelli thinly edged with white on the dorsal fin. Another

Peacock Wrasse, *Cirrhilabrus temminckii*, lives on coral reefs of Japanese, Indonesian and Australian coasts. The Peacock Blenny, *Blennis pavo*, derives its name from the prominent eye-spot on the head.

There are several floral pavoninas, all with eye-spots. Two are leguminous trees, one the Royal Peacock Flower, also called Flamboyant Tree or Barbados Pride. The second is Peacock Flower Fence, *Adenanthera pavonina*. The *Iris pavonina* is a bulbous South African plant with a blue-black spot near the base with a peacock-like eye. The Peacock Tiger Flower, *Tigridia pavonia*, from Mexico is spotted at the base of the centre of the flower. The delicate *Anemone pavonina* is from Greece, an intense

38

scarlet flower with black or navy-blue centres. *Gazania pavonina* is called the Peacock Treasure Flower.

The iridescence of the peacocks' feathers suggested the naming of Peacock Coal, and tarnished copper pyrite as Peacock Copper and Ore. The brightly coloured Pavonazzo marble is often inlaid with a fine variety of red-purple colours, but it was the greenish-black hues of the green peacock that inspired Japanese pearl divers to name the rare Akoya pearl a Peacock Pearl.

Argus was the unfortunate servant of Juno whose hundred eyes were transferred to the train of the peacock, Juno's bird. His name is now synonymous with 'Eyes'. Appropriately, the Great Argus, *Argusianus argus*, is so-called for its wonderfully ocellated plumage (eye-spots like a ball and socket, black inside brown), every feather being spotted. The male bird can reach 2.3 metres in length and its circular display is between 3.6 and 4.6 metres across. It has the longest feathers in the world, two of them in the tail, between 1.5 and 1.8 metres in length and up to 15 centimetres wide. The first specimen was brought to

A lithograph by William Hart of the Great Argus Pheasant for John Gould's magisterial seven-volume *Birds of Asia* (1850–83). The closely related male Crested Argus Pheasant is displaying in the background.

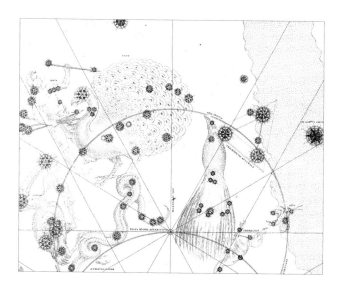

Britain from Malacca in 1780, the first live one from Singapore to London Zoo in 1872. Its close relative is the Crested Argus, *Rheinardia ocellata*, again named for the ocelli.

The *Argobuccinum argus* shell is not an obvious candidate for the name Argus, for it has brown spiral bands, rather than spots, on a lighter background. The Eyed Cowry, on the other hand, is classified as *Cypraea argus*, a description it fully deserves.

A whole group of butterflies is referred to as Argus Butterflies, and a solitary blue butterfly, very heavily spotted, is *Plebejus argus*, the Silver-studded Blue. The Argus Butterflies include two in the UK, the Brown Argus and the Northern Brown Argus, each of which has a distinctive eye-spot on the forewing in addition to the many spots on both pairs of wings.

Over the last 250 years, several other species, initially named *Pavo* or *Argus*, have lost their adjectives in subsequent reclassifying.

One of the constellations of the southern sky is called Pavo; its largest star, some 183 light years away, is called Peacock. At 19 mag. Peacock is the brightest star, not only of the constellation Pavo but in its environs, and being easy to see is useful to mariners. The constellation was seen and named at the end of the sixteenth century by Keyser and De Houtman, Dutch astronomers. It was first depicted by Johannes Bayer in his *Uranometria* of 1603, in which he showed its position in the southern sky. He engraved the word Pavo, but did not name the largest star, Peacock, in the head of the bird.

An 1860s wood engraving of the peacock butterfly. The eyespots on the wings resemble peacock-tail ocelli.

2 Unnatural History

The great divide between eastern and western philosophies and attitudes is clearly marked in relation to peacocks. Over much of the east, the bird is revered for its beauty and held sacred in association with deities, for which it is an avatar or symbol of some characteristic of the god. The attribute is a positive one, power or beauty being most common. In the west, the peacock is perceived as being vain and proud, and has been compared with a devil for its voice and likened to a thief for the manner of its walk. Only its magnificent feathers find praise, and become associated with angels' wings. In the nineteenth century even the ocelli in the train feathers were denigrated as bringing ill fortune and likened to the 'evil eye' – and there is no worse accusation than possessing the evil eye, which can bring misfortune at a glance.

The oldest myths and religious beliefs about blue peacocks belong to the Hindu religion, which was established in northern India between 1700 and 1500 BC. When village shrines were set up they were devoted to several favourite local deities. These Hindu gods and heroes are still as alive in modern India as they were when first venerated. When the sacred books, the *Rig Veda*, later *Vedas* (in Sanskrit *c.* 1500 BC) and *Upanishads*, were written few could read them but all enjoyed hearing them recited. The two great epics from these early times are still popular. The epic *Ramayana* tells of

Peacocks form a guard of honour in this *Nativity* scene from a Book of Hours, the *Heures de Charles de France*, 1473.

Rama, the incarnation of the god Vishnu, and his friend
Hanuman the monkey chieftain, setting out to recover Rama's
wife, Sita, abducted by the demon king Ravana. The peacock
played but a small role in this story, but the second great epic,
the *Mahabharata* (composed in its present form about 300 BC),
is set on the plain of the Upper Ganges, and tells of two families
fighting on an immense scale with swords and bows and arrows.
One poor victim, Dhananajaya, had 'myriads upon myriads and
millions upon millions of arrows furnished with peacock feathers' shot towards him. Several other warriors were felled by
such arrows, fletched with peacock feathers taken from the blue
peacock, which was present 4,000 years ago in immense
numbers in India.

The main Hindu gods formed a triumvirate with Brahma the
creator, Vishnu the preserver and Shiva the destroyer. Sarasvati,
wife of Brahma, is regularly worshipped in educational institu-
tions and represented with four arms, one of which carries a
book, and her mount is a peacock, occasionally a parrot. One of
Shiva's sons is Karttikeya, the god of war, whose vehicle is a peacock. All the gods have a *vahana*, a vehicle, literally an animal of
some kind on which they ride. In southern India Karttikeya is
one of the most prominent deities and has his own cult and
mythology. The gods have as many hands as are required to
carry their symbols. In a print of the young Karttikeya, he carries his spear in his right hand while the left rests around the
peacock's neck. A cobra is held in the bird's talons.

Peacocks are sacred to Lakshmi, the wife of the deity Vishnu,
and she is occasionally depicted with armbands in the form of
peacocks. She is a goddess of fertility and so is believed to be
associated with new growth. The rainy season refreshes the
landscape, hence the increased calling by Lakshmi's peacock
during the rainy season. The bird is also the cosmic mount of

Kama, the god of love, and the sacred mount of Sarawati, the goddess of poetry and wisdom.

Mayura is the Indian name for the peacock, a sacred bird, the symbol of immortality, which is believed to have been created from the feathers of a much larger bird, Garuda. The peacock is often depicted killing a snake, the symbol of cyclic time. In southern India, the discarded feathers are collected by peacock dancers who fix them in a semicircle round the upper body. The dance celebrates the peacock's sacred role in the rebirth and the unity of the cosmos. The Raj Gonds of Andhra Pradesh in Central India are noted for their fantastic headdresses of peacock feathers, made for their dancers who imitate the peacock's courtship dance.

Bundles of peacock feathers are an attribute of numerous deities, for example, Krishna, as well as being used for dusting sacred images and implements and sweeping temple floors so that no one inadvertently treads on an insect. In Darshan Hindu gurus like to use peacock feathers to deliver Shaktiput (creative force, energy) to their disciples. This is in keeping with the belief that peacocks bring harmony and joy, and their feathers in the home help to safeguard the energy in the environment.

A charming myth about Krishna, lord of the cowherds, relates how the god's attendant milkmaids first learned to dance. When young Krishna chanced upon the milkmaids bathing in the River Jumna, he decided that he liked seeing them naked and hid their saris which had been left on the riverbank. He then climbed into a tree. When the maidens emerged from the river and could not find their saris, they were puzzled, and then embarrassed when they heard and saw Krishna laughing at them. They begged him to return their saris but he refused to do so until they had joined hands and danced around him in supplication. All the damsels fell in love with him and

The Hindu warrior god Karittikeya, the son of Shiva, with his peacock mount, on a 6th-century sandstone relief from the Punjab.

wanted to hold his hand, so he had to multiply his arms as many times as necessary to hold their hands and teach them how to dance in a circle round him. The peacocks standing nearby watched the dance of the milkmaids and learned to copy their movements and to dance themselves.[1] Lord Krishna is said to have worn peacock plumes around his head.

Among the Bhils in central India, the Mori clan worship the peacock as their totem and make offerings of grain to it. *Mor* is the Hindi, Urudu, Gujarati, Punjabi and Marathi name for the peacock. At a wedding a small effigy of the bird is worshipped, but a sour note creeps in since the same clan believes that even to set foot on the tracks of a peacock in the jungle could make them suffer from some disease, and women seeing a peacock must veil their faces and look away.

Other Hindu myths are built around the idea that the peacock train is like the sky, full of stars, serene and beautiful. At times, the stars are obscured and the skies dark, just as the peacock loses its train. The analogy is also applied to the sun and the moon, which also appear, then disappear, just like the radiance of brilliant colours on the peacock's train as it unfurls it open and then furls it closed again.[2] To this day, peacocks are to be seen walking around Hindu shrines and temples, respected, even regarded with affection, but on no account to be hurt or hassled.

Buddhism is a calm and peaceful religion founded by Siddhartha Gautam, or Buddha, who was born in 563 BC. He is regarded as the wise and gracious Enlightened One, and rode on the back of a peacock, sitting in a lotus flower. He is depicted with four arms to bestow happiness and good fortune on those who believe in his power. He destroys evil and unwhole-

A purified Muhammad on his fabulous mount Buraq, from a 16th-century Turkish version of the *Siyar-i-Nahi* ('Progress of the Prophet').

some thoughts as easily as the peacock catches and eats young snakes and harmful insects. Images of the Buddha are revered and offerings made to him in Tibet, Thailand, Sri Lanka and Japan. A fan of peacock feathers is an attribute of several minor Buddhist deities of Tibet, as well as being among the sacred utensils of Lamaist rituals.

Despite it being a sacred bird, Indians once hunted and ate peacocks. One of their emperors, Asoka, *c.* 269 BC, ate them until converted to Buddhism, upon which he adopted the doctrine of *ahimsa* that forbade killing animals.

Vairocana was one of a group of five Buddhas of Meditation, often featured in the symbolic structure of stupas (dome-shaped shrines) and pagodas. The statue of Vairocana, a symbol of absolute wisdom, is at the centre, with four other statues at each cardinal point of the compass. Each statue is distinguished by its gesture, mount, attributes and the vices with which they are associated. Amitabha, at the western point of the compass, is shown with a peacock or swan, and a lotus, and represents the vice of lust.

A Nepalese deity called Janguli protects people against snakebite and poisoning. The peacock eats snakes and is thought to be able to help those suffering from snakebite in many parts of the east. Janguli is depicted riding on a peacock.

Muhammad (*c.* 570–632) was born in Mecca, Saudi Arabia, and died in Medina. He is regarded as the Messenger of Allah. His followers, Muslims, are not supposed to make any figurative art of Allah, man or animals, but there are exceptions. According to a sixteenth-century Turkish version of the *Siyar-i-Nahi* ('Progress of the Prophet'), a purified Muhammad was mounted on a fabulous creature named Buraq that had a woman's face, a mule's body, a peacock's tail and the ability to cover a distance as far as the eye could see in a single bound.

Riding Buraq (who had been ridden by other prophets before him) Muhammad passed through seven heavens and enjoyed the rarest privilege granted to any man, of seeing God's unveiled face. To Muslims, the peacock is a cosmic symbol, representing either the whole universe or the full moon or sun, when it spreads its train.

Among the Muslims of Java a myth relates that the green peacock, which guarded the gates of paradise, ate the Devil and that is how he managed to get inside. This myth makes a unity of the duality of good and evil and also explains the bird's mysterious iridescent colours. In Iraq and other parts of the Middle East, the Yezidi sect hold that the Devil is not evil and they call him the Peacock Angel, or King Peacock, and regard him as a messenger of God.

Taoism is a Chinese philosophical system founded by Lao Zi in the sixth century BC. He believed that the universe is kept in balance by the opposing forces of yin and yang. The Taoist Queen Mother of the West, Hsi Wang Mu, sometimes rides on a peacock, though more often on a crane.

At the same period, in the west, some fables, probably long narrated by itinerant storytellers, were collected and written down by a freed slave called Aesop. His fables may be defined as narratives in which animals are, for the purpose of moral instruction, made to act and speak with human interests and passions. Aesop was Greek, born in the latter half of the sixth century BC on Samos, the island reputed as a centre of learning; its most notable inhabitants also included Pythagoras and Epicurus. Aesop may have been familiar with peacocks, for they are believed to have been kept in the temple of Hera (later known as Juno), the Greek goddess, situated 9 kilometres west of the ancient capital of Samos, Pithagorio. The first temple on the site was built in the eighth century BC, and replaced by a sec-

'The Crane and the Peacock', wood engraving by Thomas Bewick from his *Select Fables* (1820).

ond in the sixth century, soon destroyed in an earthquake and in turn replaced by a third. Aesop may have known this one, or following another disastrous fire, the fourth temple on the site, built by Polykrates after *c.* 525 BC. This was never completed and the remains are what visitors see today. Coins from Samos feature a peacock riding on the prow of Hera's ships.

Aesop's fable 'The Peacock and the Crane' describes how a peacock taunted a crane with the dullness of its plumage. 'Look at my brilliant colours, and see how much finer they are than your poor feathers.' To which the crane replied: 'I do not deny that yours are far gayer than mine, but when it comes to flying, I can soar into the clouds, but you are confined to the earth like any dunghill cock.' In Aesop's day that would have been an antidote to boasting, but we know now that the peacock can fly very well, though it does not soar high or migrate like the crane.

'The Vain Jackdaw' or 'Fable of the Raven' is much more imaginative, even if later editors of Aesop cannot make up their minds as to which of the black-feathered Corvidae was intended. The story works best with a glossy black raven. Jupiter announced that he intended to appoint a king over the birds,

Pieter Casteels,
*Fable of the
Raven*, 1719,
oil on canvas.

The peacock's
complaint to
Juno, by Walter
Crane, from
'The Baby's Own
Aesop' in *Triplets*
(1899).

and named a day on which they were to appear before his throne, when he would select the most beautiful of them to be their ruler. Wishing to look their best, they gathered by the banks of a stream, where they bathed and preened their feathers. The raven, realizing that he could not compete with so many colourful birds, waited until they had all gone, then picked up the most gaudy of the feathers they had dropped (the brightest and best being those of the peacock) and fastened them about his own body, with the result that he looked more colourful than any. When the appointed day came, the birds assembled before Jupiter's throne and, after passing them in review, he was about to appoint the raven as king, when all the rest set upon the king-elect, stripped him of his borrowed plumes and exposed him for the black raven that he really was. The moral was that men in debt, like the raven, cut a dash with other people's money. Make them pay up, and they will be seen for the nobodies they really are. The literary term 'the peacock's feather', derived from this fable, means a borrowed ornament of style interpolated into a composition.

Several artists have delighted in painting their version of this fable, in which the peacock is prominent, claiming back its own feather, doubtless angry because it thought, as the most beautiful bird, it ought to be proclaimed king of the birds. It is relatively easy for an artist to make a peacock look outraged with so many feathers to ruffle and an expressive train to paint in a sweep of indignation, but Pieter Casteels's peacock is more intent on retrieving its own distinctive feather.

The peacock and Juno had a special relationship, because the peacock owed the eye-spots in the long train plumes to her. It was natural, therefore, that when the peacock had a complaint, it went back to the goddess. It was greatly discontented because it had not a beautiful voice like the nightingale. 'The nightingale's song is the envy of all the birds,' the peacock said, 'but whenever I utter a sound I become a laughing-stock.' Juno tried to be diplomatic, saying: 'You have not, it is true, the power of song, but then you far excel all the rest in beauty; your neck flashes like the emerald and your splendid tail is a marvel of gorgeous colour.' But the peacock was not appeased: 'What is the use of being beautiful with a voice like mine?' he replied. Juno became stern: 'Fate has allotted to all their destined gifts: to yourself beauty, to the eagle strength, to the nightingale song, and so on to all the rest in their degree; but you alone are dissatisfied with your portion. Make then no more complaints for if your present wish were granted, you would quickly find cause for fresh discontent.'

The gods and goddesses of Greece and Rome each had their attributes, like the older Hindu gods had their avatars, which helped to identify the characters in a painting for both the literate and illiterate. Peter Paul Rubens's painting depicts Henri IV of France receiving the portrait of Maria de' Medici, a prospective bride. This painting would have been instantly understood by his contemporaries as featuring Jupiter (because of the thunderbolt behind him) and Juno, because of the peacock beside her. The inference is that this is likely to be a marriage made in heaven. Additionally, the splendour of the peacock's feathers, with their rainbow colours, meant that it was sometimes depicted in art as a symbol of heaven.[3]

From the beginning of Christian art, a way to identify the characters of the story was to attach the symbols of Christian martyrs and saints alongside their portraits. For example, a figure holding keys was recognized as St Peter, St John the Baptist had a lamb, St Jerome a lion. No saint had a peacock; instead that bird came to symbolize a doctrine rather than a person, Christ's incorruptibility and Resurrection. This came

In Rubens's oil painting of *Henri IV Receiving the Portrait of Maria de' Medici* (1620s), Juno is identified by her peacock, which is craning its neck to look at the image of the prospective bride.

about because the peacock had gained a reputation for its flesh being incorruptible. St Augustine (AD 354–430) regarded the indestructibility of the flesh as a miracle:

> This property, when I first heard of it, seemed to me incredible but it happened at Carthage that a bird of this kind was cooked and served up to me. I took a suitable

slice of flesh from its breast, and when it had been kept as many days as make any other flesh stinking, it was produced and set before me and emitted no offensive smell . . . For who except God, the Creator of all things, endowed the flesh of the dead peacock with the power of never decaying?[4]

Peacock flesh is tough and dry meat, so if placed in the sun where it can dry thoroughly, especially after liberally sprinkling it with spices, it becomes as hard as leather. For this reason, it does not putrefy like other meats.

In the cemeteries or catacombs south of Rome dating back to the second and third centuries AD, pictures of peacocks and their feathers were drawn on the floors, walls and ceilings. The hallways of shelves with rectangular compartments for stone coffins were decorated with themes of Baptism, Eucharist and Resurrection. In typical scenes of the art of the period, the peacock was closely linked to the Eucharist by two birds flanking the cup holding the wine.

Confronting peacocks on an 11th-century Byzantine marble screen in the cathedral of S. Maria Assunta, Torcello.

Paintings of the *Annunciation* (as that by Carlo Crivelli, National Gallery, London) included a peacock to signify Christ's eventual rising from the dead. In scenes of the *Nativity of Christ*, peacocks were painted near the figure of the child to symbolize the Resurrection. It is unusual to find a whole guard of honour of peacocks (as in the illustration on p. 42); emphasizing not only the belief in incorruptibility, but also the annual moult and regrowth as a symbol of the Resurrection, plus the sapphire breast and eyed train spread out like the heavens strewn with stars. Owing to their ability to destroy serpents, peacocks were also depicted flanking the Tree of Knowledge.

Far less flattering, the peacock became a symbol of pride and vanity. Displaying its best feature so persistently and blatantly, it came to embody the sin of pride. Illustrations of the Seven Deadly Sins regularly included a peacock in the assemblage of symbolic objects. Pieter Brueghel made a series of engravings of the Seven Deadly Sins: anger, avarice, envy, gluttony, lust, pride and sloth, combining entertainment with moral instruction.

The *Sin of Pride*, one of the series of engravings after Pieter Brueghel illustrating the *Seven Deadly Sins*, published in 1556–7.

The 'peacock in his pride', that is, displaying, is prominent in his engraving of 'Pride', standing by a woman holding up a mirror. The grotesque figure in the left foreground has the suspicion of a peacock feather in its tail, as does the hatching egg figure on the right. There is also a peahen on the far right. Brueghel's contemporaries would have understood the hidden meanings of all the components of this picture, but they are largely lost to us today.

In Christian Rome during the Easter celebrations, the pope was carried into St Peter's wafting a fan made of ostrich feathers onto which were sewn cut-out ocelli from a peacock's train feather. This time, the symbolism was of the vigilance of the Church.

One belief about the peacock was shared by both east and west. The male's persistent calls were said to be a sure sign of wet weather. That the birds are more vocal in the monsoon period is because that coincides with the mating season in India and Sri Lanka. Birds calling to foretell rain is a very old superstition in the west, where birds attributed with such powers include the woodpeckers, quail and red-throated divers, among several others.

Peacocks figure largely in medicine. In a Singhalese pharmacopoeia the feather is recommended as a cure for rheumatism, sprains and dislocations. The ocellus is considered to be an excellent antidote against rat-bite. The feather must be wrapped in a piece of dried plantain leaf, set alight and then the smoke inhaled three times.

In east and west the peacock has been regarded as a royal bird, and so untouchable by ordinary men and women. When kept in temples in India where they were sacred, or temples of Hera/Juno, where they were only for the pleasure of the goddess, they were sacrosanct. To steal a feather, or worse, a bird, brought immediate and painful punishment, even death. It is thought that this may be the basic reason for the bird itself, or just its feathers, becoming regarded as unlucky.

In Britain there is a common superstition that it is unlucky to have the eyed train feathers in the house. For centuries, people of all nations have worn the feathers as personal adornments in hats, or carried them shaped into fans, and the agricultural labourers of Lincolnshire even wore them in their hats when they went to the Statute fairs to find work, buying them from hawkers. Still, the superstition persisted, especially among actors, who are terrified of having the feathers in the theatre, believing their presence will cause the play to fail. Peter Bull, the actor, wrote: 'anything to do with peacocks is fatal . . . I put on a play called "Cage me a Peacock" which lost me every penny I had'. [5]

The belief that feathers in the house caused a death is as old, if not older, than the Swiss physician Paracelsus (1493–1541) who wrote: 'if a Peacock cries more than usuall, or out of his time, it foretels the death of some in that family to whom it doth belong'. Short of foretelling a death, it might well cause the girls of the household to become old maids.[6] The ever-open eyes of the train may account for the superstition, as well as its associations with the 'evil eye', an ancient and widespread belief that certain individuals had the power to harm or even kill with a glance.

There are positive superstitions associated with the peacock, however. The *Hamdullah Al-Mostaufi Al-Qazwini* explains:

The peacock is forbidden to be eaten. It lives twenty-five years. Its cry puts to flight creeping things. Its brain eaten with rue and honey cures colic and pain in the belly. If one with griping be given its bile, a quarter of a drachm with oxymel in warm water, he will be cured; and it will loose a dumb tongue. Its flesh increases sexual power, and allays pain in the knee. If its fat be smeared over a frost-bitten limb, it will restore it. If its claw be tied on a woman in the pains of childbirth, it will relieve them immediately.[7]

How one can be forbidden to eat the bird, and then be served up with all these different parts of it, is not explained.

Protection against evil is obtained from wearing an amulet or charm. The use of amulets is widespread by believers in Buddhism, Islam and Hinduism. In Tibet an amulet is used to provide protection from malignant spirits. In Islam the most potent amulet is one with verses written from the Quran. An example of an amulet case, worn strung round the neck, was found at Nihavand with a Turkish offical's possessions. Both sides are decorated with a peacock in repoussé, surrounded by the Quranic text in Kufic script: 'He is God, One God, the Everlasting Refuge, who has not begotten, and has not been begotten, and equal to Him is not any one' (sura CXII). The text is repeated on front and back.

C. W. Beebe, who knew the birds in their native countries in the first years of the twentieth century, was scathing of the superstitions attached to them. 'In all the literature of the Greeks, Romans, Arabs and Jews, there is nothing but commendation of the peacock and unqualified admiration for its beauty,' and added: 'Silly superstitions of ill-luck of the evil eye is widespread now in the United States, England, France and Germany. There is no evidence of this in India or China.'[8]

Anthropomorphism – seeking to explain animal behaviour in human terms – led to imputing human attributes to the peacock, like pride, ostentation, strutting, foretelling weather. Curiously, associating the peacock with pride was so well established by constant repetition that this attribute of the peacock became reversed, so that a man could be described as being 'as proud as a peacock'. Few other birds have achieved a similar figure of speech.

Some households remained blessedly free of fear and superstition, and enjoyed the sheer beauty and consequent delight afforded to all owners of a peacock's train feathers. The lady sitting peacefully in a cluttered Victorian 'sweet harmonious home' (in John Atkinson Grimshaw's painting *Dulce Domum*) is unworried by the presence of peacock feather fans, and a large vase of feathers. It was painted at a time when the wearing of peacock feathers was at its peak and the Aesthetic Movement and Art Nouveau artists were using them extensively as motifs, untroubled by superstitious associations. Today, the feathers are used in large flower arrangements, to make fans, and in artwork of various kinds. Anything as exquisitely beautiful as a peacock's feather could not possibly do anyone any harm.

Thomas Bewick's wood engraving from the *Select Fables* showing the Vain Jackdaw being deprived of his false feathers by five peacocks.

3 The Blue Indian Peacock
at Home

The traditional range of the blue peacock, *Pavo cristatus*, extends from northern Pakistan eastwards south of the Himalayas, through Jammu, southern Kashmir and Nepal to Assam, south through Nagaland, Manipur and Mizoram to Chittagong, to the western bank of the Brahmaputra in Bangladesh, and all through India and Sri Lanka. From time immemorial, the blue peacock has enjoyed freedom within this vast region to roam at will through forests, villages, in sacred temples and royal palaces. In the forest, large musters of these birds range up to 900 to 1,200 metres above sea level, rarely higher, so that the colossal mountain ranges of the Karakoram and Himalayas formed a barrier to their spread northwards, while the Arakan Hills prevented them moving eastwards and so overlapping with the green peacock. The two species do not overlap anywhere.

The Indus Valley provided the earliest source of peacocks for the ancient empires of the west. This truly spectacular valley through which the Indus (the river that gave its name to the sub-continent) flows for the first part of its length in the Karakoram–Himalaya trough is fed by melt-water and then receives tributaries in such abundance that it carries at its mouth in the Arabian sea twice the volume of the Nile. The Karakorams are one of the highest mountain barriers in the

Gauri Ragini's 1610 Mughal gouache of a 'night-scene in an Indian garden' shows a peacock on the ground attacking a snake.

world, extending for some 480 kilometres from the Afghan border to the Shyok River, dividing Pakistan from China and running parallel to the Punjab Himalayas, separated only by the Indus Valley.

The Indus Valley was the area of the earliest Indian civilization, 2600–1800 BC, the Harappan, named after a major city, Harappa. This civilization was remarkably advanced, with permanent architecture of baked bricks, including large granaries, artisans' quarters with sophisticated plumbing and evidence of city planning. Indian art, painting, sculpture and architecture date back to this period. It was here also that the basic Hindu religion developed. Hindu artists created sculptures in caves and huge temple complexes.

Indus pots are often of fine quality and are mostly wheel-turned. A jar that came from a cemetery at Harappa is coloured buff, pink, red and black, and bears a group of painted peacocks, in addition to various leaf motifs. A vase from the post-Indus

An Indus pot with a peacock motif, from the ancient city of Harappa in the Punjab.

cemetery at Harappa also has a peacock within borders. Other examples, painted in black over a red surface, have been discovered in archaeological digs in the valley.[1] The Indus Valley tradition of depicting peacocks has continued down to the present, with the artists of Rajasthan still frequently representing them.

There is evidence of trade between Harappan territories, the Persian Gulf region and Mesopotamia.[2] It is believed that this most accessible part of India for early Arabian adventurers, hugging the coast as they travelled east, sheltering in bays each night, was the area from which the first peacocks reaching the Mediterranean were obtained.

The beginning of modern Hinduism developed between 1700 and 1500 BC, when the north-west of India was invaded by the light-skinned Aryans who destroyed much of the civilization of north India and established their new customs and worship of many gods. They overran the north and the Deccan plateau. Village shrines were set up all over the region, with the gods Lakshmi, Brahma and Kama each portrayed riding on peacocks.

India first became united, apart from the far south, under the Mauryan emperors of 321–184 BC, and enjoyed a period of stability and peace. The influence of Hindu beliefs and tolerance towards all living creatures ensured the prosperity of the peacocks, and as this was the age in which the spectacular temples were built across India, some peacocks were immortalized in temple carvings throughout the region. Hinduism advanced further in central and southern India. Figures of royal peacocks from the ancient Hindu epic of *Ramayana* were carved in the temple at Nrusinghanath; more peacocks with figures of monkeys were sculpted in the tenth-century AD temple at Bhubanaswar; and in a Brahma temple at Pushkar, peacocks, the vehicle of Lord Brahma's consort, adorn the temple walls. About AD 200, the Greek Aelian had heard about peacocks in

A 14th-century Deccan bronze peacock, a favourite image in Indian art.

India and wrote that in the parks of royal residences there 'tame peacocks and pheasants are kept and they live in the cultivated shrubs to which the royal gardeners pay due attention'.[3]

In the first century AD, according to a long-standing tradition, the doubting apostle Thomas conducted missionary work in India. He is also believed to have died there. Marco Polo visited his chapel at Mylapore (i.e. 'city of peacocks') or Mailapur, when on his homeward journey from China about 1290–93. Marco Polo related the story of the saint saying his prayers outside his hermitage, surrounded by peacocks, being accidentally shot by a hunter out with his bows and arrows to shoot peacocks. Having been struck by an arrow in his right side, Thomas died from his wound. A chapel was built in his honour and Marco Polo said that both Christians and Saracens 'greatly frequented it in pilgrimage', for the Saracens held the saint in great reverence. The small town later became engulfed by the city of Madras (Chennai).

Following Marco Polo, hundreds of adventurers, traders and entrepreneurs journeyed to India to seek commercial agreements with the maharajas or to serve them as physicians, artists and mercenaries. Missionaries also visited, such as Jordanus of Severac, a French Dominican who landed in India in 1321 and wrote home describing elephants, rhinoceroses, lynx and flying foxes among the native quadrupeds, kites and peacocks among the birds.

The Mughal era was initiated in 1526 when Babur, a warrior prince of a small Central Asian kingdom, defeated Lodi, ruler of Delhi. Babur's successful military exploits in India, as well as those of his son Hamayun and then Akbar (ruled 1556–1605), led to the formation of an empire that encompassed almost all of the sub-

Peacock in a Rainstorm at Night, a late 16th-century Deccan painting. The portrayal is fanciful: peacocks do not fly in the rain, or at night.

continent, except its most southern part. Akbar and his relations, the rajputs who established their grip on the different states and small kingdoms, built thick-walled citadels or forts, within which were their palaces, courts, gardens and menageries – everything for a life of comfort in secure surroundings. One such palace built at Udaipur, now called the City Palace, was in a perfect setting overlooking Lake Pichola. The most elaborate of several interior courts, in the private zone, was Mor Chowk, or the Peacock Court. It was named after the birds modelled in high relief and adorned with coloured glass that were set into the walls.

Having established themselves in safety in their forts and palaces, the Mughal emperors turned their attention to the arts. Mughal court artists excelled in miniature painting, particularly in the reigns of Akbar, his son Jahangir (1605–27) and Shah Jehan (1628–58). Their subjects ranged from portraits and histories to birds, mammals and flowers. Akbar was a patron of the arts and had favourite painters of great virtuosity and naturalism from all religious groups and ranks of society. Some hundred artists, both native Indians and others from conquests, who trained apprentices, worked on illustrations for manuscripts and compositions that were kept in albums. Among Akbar's favourites was Basawan who painted a delightful minature of *The Foppish Dervish Rebuked* by a wise and holy Sufi. The dervish was stitching a new garment for himself when a passing Sufi rebuked him, saying 'That robe is your God.' Basawan emphasized the point by painting a richly clad peacock on the balcony. The peacock has turned its back on the Sufi, indicating that his rebuke will be ignored. Another favourite, Miskin, perhaps Akbar's greatest artist, painted a picture of Noah's Ark, crowded on four decks with animals. Birds were on the top deck, including a peacock. Akbar loved animal paintings, so Miskin's *The Raven Addressing the Assembled Animals* gave him another opportunity to bring together a large group, with fishes in the sea at the bottom of a mountain being scaled by snakes and quadrupeds and a dragon. The two peacocks are low down the mountain, the male looking very concerned at the raised hood of a large cobra. There is a sense of mischief and humour in these miniatures that is very engaging.

A later painting, of *Two Lovers on a Terrace*, gazing into one another's eyes, by Bal Chand, *c.* 1633, includes a servant girl wafting a peacock feather fly-swat or fan. Many pictures of palace interiors show large bunches of peacock train feathers in containers, ready for use as fans.

Jahangir's most famous artist was Ustad Mansur. A lively album portrait of *Peafowl*, painted *c.* 1610, is attributed to him. Most of the western paintings of peafowl show them static, so this male bird, which has run forwards to stab at a small snake that it is now eating, is an unusual, lively portrait. Great care was taken with his powerful legs (one of which Mansur has had to paint several times, to get the correct angle), and with the tense female. It is not only masterly but refreshing in depicting characteristic poses of the birds.

A servant wafts a peacock feather over *Two Lovers on a Terrace* in an album painting by Bal Chaud. Prince Shah Shuja, the second son of Shah Jehan, married the daughter of a courtier and wit related to the royal house of Iran.

Akbar was visited in 1599 by Sir John Mildenhall at the behest of a group of London merchants who had formed an association in order to trade directly with India. At this time rival European powers controlled the East India trade and thus the price of valuable spices. Elizabeth I sent the delegation, led by Sir John, to negotiate with Akbar to obtain privileges for this venture. Mildenhall succeeded and the establishment by royal charter of the East India Company on 31 December 1600 led to three-and-a-half centuries not only of trade but, later, colonization.

The Mughal Empire may have reached its peak under Akbar, but Shah Jehan has become more famous for the beautiful Taj Mahal that he built for his wife. He was an extravagant builder all over the Mughal empire. Apart from the Taj Mahal (*c.* 1632–47), he built new palaces inside the forts at Lahore and Agra, the Great Mosque at Agra and a new palace and city at Delhi, which became his capital. An order was placed by Shah Jehan in 1629 for a peacock throne to be made for his palace at Delhi. It was sited in the middle of the Diwan-i Khass, a hall for private

An early 17th-century depiction of peafowl by the Mughal painter Ustad Mansur.

audiences and durbars or assemblies. Shah Jahan used the Diwan-i Khass to consult with his wazir and the highest officers and provincial governors. During his reign, on Wednesdays, courts of law assembled in the Diwan-i Khass before the throne. The throne was a small jewelled pavilion surmounted by a golden arch with a pair of gold peacocks on the roof. It was studded with the finest rubies, emeralds and pearls. Peacock feathers were held in vases by the throne. The presence of a raja (Indian prince or king) was signified by a standard made of peacock feathers, among other trappings.

A Mughal painting of the 17th-century ruler Shah Jehan on his peacock throne.

The line of strong Mughal rulers came to an end about 1707 and the empire fell apart quickly. India became vulnerable to outside attacks and during one snatch and grab raid, by a Persian army under Nadir Shah in 1739, Delhi was sacked, and the peacock throne was seized and taken to Persia. Henry Rawlinson saw it there in 1837 on a visit to Muhammad Shah, when he was stationed in Tehran, describing 'probably the most splendid apartment in Persia, the focus being the magnificent 17th century Peacock throne with its 26,000 emeralds, rubies, diamonds and pearls'. The throne has since disappeared.[4] During the period of chaos, with invading armies and states manoeuvring for position, the competing traders of the British East India Company and the French equivalent joined in the affrays. The British took the opportunity to oust the French, then systematically annexed the Mughal territories during the course of the eighteenth century.

Two East India Company servants, serving in India, took home with them deep impressions of Indian architecture that they incorporated in new houses built for them in England. Their knowledge of Indian architecture was shared by Thomas Daniell, the artist. Daniell (1749–1840) travelled in India with his nephew William for a decade following their arrival in 1784. They painted scenes and buildings, and on their return home published *Oriental Scenery* with aquatint illustrations. An architect, Samuel Pepys Cockerell (1754–1827), was inspired by *Oriental Scenery* to create the designs for Sezincote, Gloucestershire, first bought by Colonel John Cockerell in 1795 on his return from Bengal, then inherited by his youngest brother Charles Cockerell, a surveyor to the East India Company, in 1798. Cockerell and Thomas Daniell worked together on the plans, creating arches in the shape of peacocks' raised trains over the first-floor windows on the south front. They would have reminded the owner of the peacocks that decorated so many buildings in Rajasthan. In addition, by 1805 a

Peacock arches at Sezincote, Gloucestershire, an Indian-style country house by S. P. Cockerell, 1803.

long curving conservatory, part of which housed exotic birds, had been built with more peacock train arches. The Prince Regent visited Sezincote about 1807 and is thought to have been influenced by the Indian style when he remodelled Brighton Pavilion. Similar Indian motifs occur in the house built nearby at Daylesford, Worcestershire, for John Cockerell's more famous friend Warren Hastings.

As the East India Company secured successive states, missionaries followed in their wake, and the Church of England established dioceses across the country. Some British clergymen in India took an interest in its natural history. It is obvious from the way in which he describes a blue peacock taking off, like a jump-jet Harrier, that Bishop Heber had closely observed the living birds:

> With pendant train and rustling wings
> Aloft the gorgeous peacock springs;
> And he, the bird of hundred dyes,
> Whose plumes the dames of Ava prize.

The Reverend Reginald Heber (1783–1826) was an English divine and hymn writer, inducted into the family living at Hodnet in Shropshire. He accepted the see of Calcutta in 1823, but died at Trichinopoly, near Madras, three years later. He had first-hand experience of peacocks in India, hence the vivid description of them.[5]

Magnificent fortified residences continued to be built by the Rajput rulers of western and central India in the eighteenth century. These princes were in the service of the Delhi emperor, consequently their architecture was influenced by that of the Mughals. A remarkable example, with a superb peacock door surround, was built by Sawai Jai Singh, founder of Jaipur, Rajasthan, in his royal residence completed in 1733. Ornate brass doors in the peripheral wall of one court are surmounted by panels with brightly coloured peacocks. Five displaying birds form an arch over the doors. Two further peacocks in the top corners of the frame round the door act as mounts for small figures.

From 1756, when the East India Company ruled Bengal and Carnatic, it extended its influence to all India. The great Indian princes, the maharajas, were obliged to accept this foreign rule and were forbidden to maintain independent armies. They were left in place in their forts, ruling over their states, subject to British control. One way in which they could affirm their royal status was by building large opulent modern residences. The princes enjoyed more security now that they were not constantly warring to maintain their borders against other potentates. In addition, they could safely enjoy sports outside their forts, such as tiger and peacock shooting.

Eating peacocks was not done by Hindus, but members of other faiths were not averse to peacock on the menu. In the nineteenth century Indian cooks even experimented with the idea of placing various animals inside one another and then

Brass doors surrounded by tilework form displaying peacocks in an inner court at Jaipur, a Rajput palatial fort completed in 1733. In the upper corners the god Karittikeya rides a peacock.

cooking the whole parcel in a hole in the ground, steaming it slowly for a long time. They began with a camel, and put inside it a goat, inside that a peacock, then a chicken, sandgrouse, quail and finally a sparrow in the centre. Exotic fare for indulgent princes was the norm within the magnificent palaces.

The British administrators and militia living in India enjoyed game-bird shooting. In 1867 William Tegetmeier wrote:

Though it cannot be said to be a favourite game with sportsmen in India, few can resist a shot at a fine peacock whirring past when hunting for small game: yet pea-chicks are well worth a morning's shikar [hunting] for the table, and a plump young peahen, if kept for two or three days, is really excellent. An old peacock is only fit to make soup of. A bird merely winged will often escape by the fleetness of its running. They generally roost on particular trees, and by going early or late to this place, they can readily be shot.[6]

There must have been many stories told in the mess at the end of a day's sport, but few would better the account of one colonel. While stalking a peacock, he was surprised to find that he had approached unusually close to this wary bird, normally clever at avoiding observation and pursuit, and not allowing an approach within gunshot. The bird ignored him and gazed intently on a small patch of jungle just in front of it. The colonel then noticed a leopard stealthily crawling on its belly toward the peacock. He was puzzled, not having heard of leopards in the neighbourhood. He raised his gun and covered the leopard. To his astonishment, it suddenly reared up, threw up both its front paws and shrieked in a voice hoarse with terror, 'Nehin Sahib, Nehin Sahib, mut chulao' (No sir, no sir, do not fire). He thought for a moment that he must be going mad, until he saw a man very cleverly got up in a leopard skin, with a well-stuffed head, and a bow and arrow in one paw, standing before him.[7] The natives were skilled at tracking and killing peacock; other fowlers caught them in snares by imitating the cry of the males.

As late as the twentieth century the maharajas created new cities, such as the one at Mysore in southern India. A new palace had been built there in the early years of the nineteenth century,

Peacocks in stained glass in the Kalyan Mandapa ('Wedding Hall') in Mysore Palace, designed by Henry Irwin in 1897.

later extended in 1932. It was unique in making use of cast-iron for two of its great state rooms, and employing a British architect. The cast-iron pillars and roof were manufactured in Glasgow by Walter Macfarlane and company of the Saracen Foundry, and shipped to Mysore. Henry Irwin designed the two halls, and decoration, including the peacock. Stained glass was in fashion in Britain and Irwin used this to decorate the halls, creating another innovation in Indian architecture.

The most famous British author to write about India was Rudyard Kipling. He barely mentioned peacocks, even in the Mowgli stories, but a haunting poem, 'The Story of the Little Hunter', has a passing reference:

> Ere Mor the Peacock flutters, ere the Monkey People cry,
> Ere Chil the Kite swoops down a furlong sheer,

Through the Jungle very softly flits a shadow and a sigh –
He is Fear, O Little Hunter, he is Fear!

In 1903 the Viceroy of India, Lord Curzon, and his wife attended an evening ball following the Coronation Durbar in Delhi. Mary, Lady Curzon wore a remarkably ornate and very heavy gown, from material embroidered by Indian craftsmen with metal thread and jewels on cloth of gold in a pattern of peacock feathers. The dress glistened in the evening lights, especially the eye of each feather that was represented by the wing case of an iridescent green beetle. The dress had been made by Worth of Paris, and may still be viewed at Kedleston Hall in Derbyshire.

In 1947 India was partitioned and the British left. The Indus Valley, the cradle of Indian civilization, was divided off to form Pakistan, where the blue peacock is today struggling for survival, there being little protection afforded it. As always, in Hindu India the birds fare better, but even there, with the breakdown of old values and beliefs, life is becoming increasingly insecure for the Indian blue peacock. The best hope for its preservation lies within secure national parks, of which there are now several. Worldwide public awareness of birds was promoted at an ornithological conference held in Tokyo in 1960 by a proposal that each country should formally designate a species as its national bird. In January 1963 India chose the blue peacock, giving a powerful incentive to protect it.[8]

SRI LANKA

As early as the fifth century BC, Roman sailors trading in the Far East went down the west coast of India and round to the next landfall, the busy port of Galle on the west coast of Sri Lanka (formerly called Ceylon), before crossing the Bay of Bengal.

They were searching for gold and tin from Sri Lanka and for spices from the Malay Peninsula and Burma.[9] Galle, a Sinhalese word meaning rocks, is situated on a rocky promontory lying to the west of a bay that opens to the south. It is a seaport with a very long history.[10] About 543 BC Wijeya, a prince of northern India, invaded and conquered Sri Lanka. Remarkably, a small remnant of descendants of the native population that Wijeya subdued, the Veddas, still survives. Vedda tribesmen were found living in a small area in the remote interior of the island in the 1930s, still using bows and arrows. They used heron, hawk and peacock feathers on their arrows.

We have few written accounts of peacocks in Ceylon, so a graphic account of them living freely in their native forest, made by Sir James Emerson Tennent in 1860, is valuable.

> As one emerges from the deep shade and approaches the park-like openings on the verge of the low country, quantities of pea-fowl are to be found either feeding on the seeds and fallen nuts among the long grass or sunning themselves on the branches of the surrounding trees. Nothing to be met with in English demesnes can give an adequate idea of the size and magnificence of this bird when seen in his native solitudes. Here he generally selects some projecting branch, from which his plumage may hang free of the foliage . . . or spreads it in the morning sun to drive off the damps and dews of the night. In some of the unfrequented portions of the eastern province, to which Europeans rarely resort, and when the pea-fowl are unmolested by the natives, their number is so extraordinary that, regarded as game, it ceases to be 'sport' to destroy them; and their cries at early dawn are so tumultuous and incessant as to banish sleep, and amount to an

William Logsdail's portrait *Lady Curzon, Viceraine of India*, at the Coronation Durbar ball in Delhi, 1903, shows her gown covered in cloth-of-gold peacock feathers.

actual inconvenience. Their flesh is excellent when served up hot, though it is said to be indigestible; but, when cold, it contracts a reddish and disagreeable thing.[11]

The struggle between the Tamil Tigers and the majority forces in Sri Lanka has done little to conserve the environment or the bird inhabitants of Sri Lanka (the name adopted in 1972, meaning Resplendent Island). The full impact of the civil war on the fauna of the island is not known.

NEPAL AND TIBET

The peacock is represented in the temples of Hindu Nepal and Buddhist Tibet, as in India, for it is a symbol of good luck, prosperity and longevity for both Hindus and Buddhists and is deified as Maha-Mayuri, the Great Peacock. Images of Tibetan Buddhist deities were adorned with precious jewellery encrusted with gems. Another association with the peacock as protector takes the form of a peacock-feather umbrella under which Palden Lhamo (the dark blue protector of all Tibetan Buddhist denominations) shelters while riding her mule through a burning sea of blood.

A visitor to this region would once have seen peacocks among the great quantities of jewellery worn by all members of society on a daily basis. This was made of turquoise, coral, lapis lazuli and pearls, set in silver and gold. Tibet was rich in gold and precious stones, which were used on ceremonial swords and sacred vessels as well as for personal adornment. Turquoise is the favourite stone and ranks second only to gold as a valuable material for jewellery.

In Newar, Nepal, jewellery is worn to mark each stage of a person's life in the belief that it gives them protection and has health-giving properties. Celebrations at birth and marriage, in

Ceremonial jewellery of the Newar people of Nepal, in silver gilt, turquoise, beryl, rubies, sapphires, diamonds, hessonite garnet and lapis lazuli.

particular, called for all the family jewels to be worn. The jew-ellers were of a high caste and highly regarded.

In Tibet peacock feathers are used in the Buddhist rituals associated with purifying water. Peacocks are symbols of com-passion and immortality, believed to provide an antidote against poison (since they eat snakes) and so became associated with the ability to neutralize the poisonous human emotions of anger and greed. A classic Tibetan story is *Goldenglow the Peacock in the Poison Grove*, by Dharmarakshita. This peacock, a king among peacocks with 500 followers, lived on the southern slope of Kailash. The wife of King Brahmadatta of Benares heard and saw the peacock and asked the king to bring it to her. His ser-

vants found the bird but could not snare it, and when confront-
ed by the peacock they explained that they would die if they
could not take it to court. The bird agreed to attend the king,
after he had prepared a suitable reception for him. With all due
ceremony, the King of the Peacocks then went to the court of
the king and all his court paid him homage. King Brahmadatta
honoured the peacock daily, making offerings and bowing to
him. Finding he could not do so one day, he allotted the task to
the queen, and she performed it for a while. She was having an
affair with a courtier, found she was pregnant and sought to kill
the peacock by poison lest he reveal the truth to the king.
However, the King of the Peacocks became even more lovely
and resplendent and told the queen that she could never kill
him with poison, and that her husband would find her out and
kill her. She fainted, wasted away and died.

The story ends with the sentence 'The King of Benares is
now Shariputra, and I [Buddha] was Goldenglow, King of the
Peacocks.'[12] The peacock is credited here with the ability to neutralize black aconite (*Aconitum ferox*), or wolf-bane, among
other poisons.

BLUE PEACOCKS TAKEN NORTH

The Singhalese ambassadors who arrived at Rome in the
reign of Emperor Claudius [AD 41–54] stated that their
ancestors had reached China by traversing India and the
Himalayan mountains long before ships had attempted
the voyage by sea and as late as the 5th century AD the King
of Ceylon in an address delivered by his envoy to the
Emperor of China shows that both routes were then in use.
It is not, however, till after the third century AD that we
find authentic records of such journeys in the literature of

China. Buddhist pilgrims, who resorted to India, published on their return itineraries and descriptions of distant countries they had visited.[13]

Merchants were attracted to Sri Lanka by trade. Chinese junks from AD 317 to 419, called at Galle for rice, vegetables, aloes-wood, sandalwood, ebony, camphor, areca-beans, sesamum, coconuts, peppers, sugar cane, myrrh, frankincense oil and drugs. They also traded in ivory and hundreds of statues of Buddha, pearls, corals, crystals, rubies, sapphires and amethysts. The island was rich in commodities desired both in the east and the west.

The earliest embassy from Sri Lanka to China was recorded in Chinese annals at the beginning of the fifth century AD. It had arrived overland by way of India, taking ten years to reach the capital of China. The kings of Sri Lanka in the sixth century acknowledged themselves vassals of the emperor of China and in 515 tribute was sent to China, a practice that continued for centuries. This proves the movement of goods and people from Ceylon and India, across the Himalayas and north through to China. There is no mention of peacocks, but they may have been taken north or, more probably, their feathers were traded. At this period, Yunnan with its indigenous green peacocks was not yet a part of the Chinese empire and was determinedly maintaining its independence. The earliest Chinese knowledge of peacocks might have been of the blue species. It would require detailed and dated Chinese pictures of both birds to verify which species was known at which period in China.

4 The Blue Indian Peacock Goes West

Naturally, the blue peacock is a sedentary bird. It does not migrate and is reluctant to fly great distances. Given sufficient food and a good roosting tree, it is comfortable in a small territory. An individual will wander further afield occasionally, but the majority of the family group will remain within a defined area. It is all the more remarkable, therefore, that this stay-at-home bird was found 5,000 kilometres away by sea from its Indian homelands, living on the eastern seaboard of the Mediterranean, as many as 3,000 years ago. Its spread is entirely due to man's intervention.

The biblical account of King Solomon importing peacocks about 950 BC is the first record of the presence of peacocks being taken westwards. From the Middle East they gradually moved further west into Europe and North America. The route from the blue peacock's native India to ancient civilized nations can be traced if we follow the route taken by traders carrying Indian gold, jewels, ivory, ebony and spices. The Indus Valley civilization that prospered in the area of modern Pakistan was already trading with cities in southern Mesopotamia around 2300 BC. The Indus Valley was an area where peafowl were plentiful, so they could have been traded by sea via the Persian Gulf, even before the time of King Solomon.

A peacock in flight.

Phoenician traders introduced peacocks, in the time of Solomon, to present-day Syria. Phoenicia (the empire flourished from 1200 to 332 BC) was the ancient Greek name for North Canaan on the east coast of the Mediterranean, including the seaboard of Lebanon and Syria.[1] Phoenician trade was both extensive and abundant. A comprehensive account is given in the Bible (Ezekiel 27, 3–25) mentioning trade with Egypt, Persia, Cyprus, Nubia, Turkey, Greece, Mesopotamia, Arabia and Africa, as well as India. The peacocks travelling to the court of King Solomon arrived in ships that had been piloted by sailors of his neighbour Hiram, King of Tyre (modern Lebanon), in Phoenicia. With Solomon's Judah, Tyre traded wood and metals in exchange for agricultural products, oil and perfumes. Solomon lived in Jerusalem, about 160 kilometres south of Tyre, and traded on the eastern Mediterranean where Hiram also traded. In 947 BC Hiram 'sent him by the hands of his servants ships, and servants that had knowledge of the sea; and they went, with the servants of Solomon to Ophir, and took thence 450 talents of gold and brought them to king Solomon'.[2] This joint expedition sailed down the Gulf of Aqaba into the Red Sea and round to Mozambique (Ophir). Solomon had built a port at the head of the Gulf of Aqaba, giving access to the Red Sea, and called it Ezion-geber. His ships put into harbours on the western and eastern coasts of the Gulf of Aqaba, calling at ports in Punt (Ethiopia) on the west and Sheba (South Yemen) on the east.[3] A sea route round to the Persian Gulf linked with trade from the east, including the Indus Valley. Solomon controlled the largest land empire in the Near East, including the termini of trading routes used by the caravans of Sheba. Blue peacocks would have reached Solomon via his ships calling in at Sheba, where he linked his trade in gold and spices with that of the Queen of Sheba. The kingdom of Saba (Sheba) extended on both sides of the Red Sea, in Ethiopia and South Yemen around this period.[4] Sabaean wealth was derived from frankincense trees (their habitat was restricted to Dhofar) and myrrh trees used for incense in ceremonies of several different religions. Myrrh was also used to prepare bodies for burial, and both myrrh and frankincense were used in medicine. The expedition was repeated, 'For the King's ships went to Tarshish with the servants of Hiram: once in every three years came the ships of Tarshish bringing gold and silver, ivory, and apes, and peacocks.'

This source of wealth and peacocks was blocked in the time of Jehoshaphat (ruler of Judah, 873–849 BC), who 'made ships of Tharshish to go to Ophir for gold but they went not; for the ships were broken at Ezion-geber'. Approximately a century later, inhabitants of the Holy Land still had knowledge of peacocks, for Job asked God: 'Gavest thou the goodly wings unto the peacocks?'[5]

From India, the peacock reached Mesopotamia, the land between the Euphrates and Tigris, now part of Iraq, in the late eighth century BC.[6] About the same time, Tiglath-Pileser III, King of Assyria (745–727 BC), whose capital was at Nineveh in Babylon, received peacocks as tribute from Arabia.

The Persian Empire, founded by Cyrus the Great in 550 BC, was expanded under his son Darius (529–485 BC) to include Afghanistan and north-west India, giving direct access to the blue Indian peacocks. The war with Greece ended Persian dominance in the ancient world, and in 331 BC Alexander the Great drove the Persians, under Darius III, to retreat on the Tigris, marking the end of the Persian and beginning of the Hellenistic period.[7] It has been said that Alexander, pupil of Aristotle (384–322 BC), the Greek philosopher, took peacocks to Greece. However, peafowl were already well known in Greece by the time of Aristotle, where they were protected because of their beauty, and orders were issued that forbade people to kill them.[8] Phoenician traders had carried the peacocks into Greece overland from Persia, Media and Babylonia, perhaps first to the island of Samos.

We do not know the exact date when the peacock was established at Hera's temple on Samos. Built to honour the goddess Hera by Polykrates, it was four times the size of the Parthenon in Athens and was talked of as the eighth wonder of the world. Antiphanes wrote that Hera 'in Samos has the golden kind of bird, the peacock that we gaze on for its beauty'.[9] Samos revolted from Athenian hegemony in 440 BC, provoking an invasion of the island, which could have provided the opportunity for the Athenians to plunder peacocks. The birds were such a rare spectacle that when taken to Athens they provoked great interest and were referred to in many passages in the Comic poets. Aristophanes (*c*. 448–*c*. 380 BC) mentioned peafowl in his comedy *Birds*.[10]

The orator Antiphon (*c*. 480–411 BC) told of a rich Athenian bird-fancier called Demos who was so overwhelmed by visitors from as far afield as Lacedaemon and Thessaly to see his peafowl and purchase their eggs that he resorted to appointing a single day a month, the day of the new moon, on which he would receive visitors. Antiphon found it impossible to tame his birds and breed from them, because they kept flying away and he could not clip their wings or he would ruin their appearance. They remained scarce, only gradually increasing in numbers until, in the mid-400s BC, Antiphanes reported that 'Once it was something grand to possess even *one* pair of peafowl, now they are commoner than quails!'[11] Heliopolis was another Greek city that was linked to the bird when it adopted a peacock emblem for the city. St Barbara, born in Heliopolis, has a peacock symbol as one of her attributes.

Alexander the Great was impressed by the peacocks he saw while campaigning as far as the Indus. He afforded them protection and would doubtless have established a muster at Alexandria after he founded that city in 333 BC, had he not died while still campaigning. It was left to the Ptolemy dynasty, which ruled over Egypt from the death of Alexander in 323 BC until the Roman conquest, to establish the birds at Alexandria. Ptolemy I founded a huge zoo at Alexandria and this was continued and enlarged by Ptolemy II. One of the processions to show off the king's possessions, held on the Feast of Dionysius in the early 270s BC, took all day to pass the stadium in Alexandria. It included 8 pairs of ostriches in harness, peacocks carried in cages, guinea fowls, pheasants, 90 elephants, 24 lions, 14 leopards, 16 panthers and still more quadrupeds.[12] One of the Ptolemies, on receiving a peacock from India, dedicated it to Zeus Polieus. Some terracotta figurines of peacocks are extant from this period and a peacock was included in a mosaic floor in a Roman house in Alexandria at Kom el-Dikka, the 'Villa of Birds'. Several museums, in Cairo and elsewhere in

Egypt, have representations of peacocks from tombs, as bronzes, in textiles, and pottery.

Aristotle was one of the earliest authors to write down what was then known of natural history. Some details appear to have been compiled from close observation of breeding pairs of peacocks, but his most pleasing observation was: 'The bird moults when the earliest trees are shedding their leaves, and recovers its plumage when the same trees are recovering their foliage.'[13] Diodorus, a Sicilian contemporary of Julius Caesar, wrote *Bibliotheke historike*, a history of the world from mythical times to Caesar's conquest of Gaul. Diodorus mentioned the presence of peacocks in Babylon. In the first century BC, rulers of Asia Minor, the Asian part of present-day Turkey, often kept them in parks and gardens.

From this scattered evidence it is clear that the peacock was known across a wide area of the Middle East. They, and their feathers, were regarded as desirable luxuries. During the rise and fall of empires, as armies invaded, the peacocks would either have been taken away with the loot or escaped into the surrounding countryside, where they might have survived if the conditions were not too inclement.

Following the discovery of the monsoon winds by the Greek merchant Hippalus in the first century AD, trading voyages in the Red Sea and Indian Ocean became commonplace. 'Roman merchants sold their wares from permanent trading stations like the one at Arikamedu on the Bay of Bengal and Roman products, occasionally Roman subjects, could be found as far afield as South-East Asia and China.'[14]

It was while the Romans had direct access to Indian peacocks that western attitudes to peacocks changed. There is no evidence to show that the Greeks had eaten peacocks, but the Romans ate them. Hortensius first served them up at an enter-

A peacock on a Roman coin of the emperor Domitian (AD 81–96).

tainment in Rome; and from that time they were considered as one of the greatest ornaments of every feast.[15] The bird was skinned, its head, neck and legs protected while cooking, then re-dressed when ready for the table. Hortensius was a Roman consul in 69 BC and in his day the peacock's train feathers were also being used to provide fly-flaps or fly-swats at banquets.

Pliny named Aufidius Hurco as being the first who fattened up peacocks for the luxurious feasts of the wealthy. In order to provide peacocks in sufficient numbers for feasts, they were bred on the small islands surrounding Italy, such as the Isle of Pianosa. Peacocks dislike flying long distances, so it was safe to allow them to roam freely on the islands where they picked up their own food and bred unmolested by predators. All their keeper had to do was to provide a daily supplement of barley. Marcus Terentius Varro (116–27 BC) explained the system in his work *On Agriculture*, whose text indicates the Roman use and exploitation of the bird in contradistinction to the Greeks' protective policies. A Roman entrepreneur, Lurco, made great profits in the fattening and sale of peacocks for the table. Varro was greatly impressed by the prices Lurco obtained for both the peafowl and their eggs.[16]

One of the most gluttonous Roman emperors, Aulus Vitellius, was emperor for only nine months in AD 69, but when he first arrived in Rome from the provinces a celebratory banquet was served by his brother with 2,000 fish and 7,000 birds. This was exceeded by Vitellius himself with a dish he described as 'the Shield of Minerva, the Guardian of the City' because of its colossal size. It included the livers of wrasse, pheasants' and peacocks' brains, flamingos' tongues and the roes of moray eels. He was a compulsive eater, even when sacrificing to the gods he robbed the altar of anything edible, and could not resist gobbling it down himself.

Bassianus, emperor of Rome from AD 218–222 was noted for serving peacocks' tongues, hearts and brains at his feasts along with flamingo heads and crests cut from live cocks. The practice of serving peacocks at Roman feasts had become so widespread that this status symbol of Roman dignitaries no doubt accompanied them as they conquered and spread throughout European countries. A lone voice was raised against this slaughter. Martial, a poet born in Spain who went to Rome in AD 64, wrote: 'You marvel whenever it opens its spectacular wings, how anyone could be so hard-hearted as to give this bird to a cook.'[17] Eventually demand outpaced production and farms were established on the Italian mainland. Writers of the day recorded the programmes for the birds' care and maintenance in great detail.

Evidence of the widespread distribution of peacocks throughout Italy in the Roman period is found on pottery hand lamps, metal statuettes, mosaics and wall paintings. In the gardens of the wealthy in the first century AD, it became fashionable to insert marble fountains and basins, sometimes in semi-circular recesses in the walls, lined with mosaics. On coins, the peacock appeared for more than a century on the aureus of

Roman mosaic of a peacock in the vaulting of the church at Beligna, 5th century AD.

Julia Titi AD 89, on billon tetradrachma of Antonius Pius of AD 176, and on a silver denarius of his wife Faustinia, of AD 141. An example of a Roman emperor giving a diplomatic gift to Greeks occurred in AD 117 when Hadrian presented a magnificent peacock of gold and jewels to the Heraion in the Corinthian district.

At the end of the second century in Rome, there were so many peafowl that they were available for all the wealthy citizens. Lucian, in a dialogue in his *Navigium*, made one of his characters fantasize that if he 'ever became rich, his ambition would be to have a peacock from India for his table'. Everyone by this time was aware of the source of these birds, and that they were still being imported from India by way of the Red Sea, perhaps also via Persia.[18]

Claudius Aelian, writing 'On Animals' *c.* AD 200, imaginatively recorded what he thought he knew about peacocks:

The Peacock knows that it is the most beautiful of birds; it knows too wherein its beauty resides; it prides itself on this and is haughty, and gathers confidence from the plumes which are its ornament and which inspire strangers with terror. In summertime they afford it a covering of its own, unsought, not adventitious. If, for instance, it wants to scare somebody it raises its tail-feathers and shakes them and emits a scream, and the bystanders are terrified, as though scared by the clang of a hoplite's [a heavily armed Greek soldier] armour. And it raises its head and nods most pompously, as though it were shaking a triple plume at one. When, however, it needs to cool itself it raises its feathers, inclines them in a forward direction and displays a natural shade from its own body, and wards off the fierceness of the sun's rays. But if there is a wind behind it, it gradually expands its feathers, and the breeze which streams through them, blowing gently and agreeably, enables the bird to cool itself. It knows when it has been praised, and as some handsome boy or lovely woman displays that feature which excels the rest, so does the Peacock raise its feathers in orderly succession; and it resembles a flowery meadow or a picture made beautiful by the many hues of the paint, and painters must be prepared to sweat in order to represent its special characteristics. And it proves how ungrudgingly it exhibits itself by permitting bystanders to take their fill of gazing, as it turns itself about and industriously shows off the diversity of its plumage, displaying with the utmost pride an array surpassing the garments of the Medes and the embroideries of the Persians.[19]

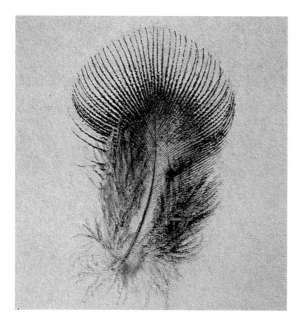

A watercolour by John Ruskin, who echoed the Roman naturalist Aelian in 1875, writing: 'I have to draw a peacock's breast feather without having heaven to dip my brush in.'

At its peak, under Trajan (*c.* AD 53–117), the Roman Empire extended from Britain to Mesopotamia and the Caspian Sea. Throughout the Roman occupation, peacocks may have been present in England. Some Roman mosaic floors in Britain include small pictures of peacocks. Examples are the Keynsham mosaic, near Bath, from one of the greatest of the Roman villas, and the Woodchester mosaic, the largest mosaic known from Roman Britain, which has an inner ring surrounding water, occupied by Orpheus, a peacock and other birds.

After the fall of the Roman Empire, Charlemagne (742–814), who conquered most of western Christendom, is said to have kept peacocks and pheasants on his estates and served thousands of peacocks at a single state banquet. For the first ten centuries AD there is little other evidence for the presence of peacocks in European countries apart from a few references gleaned from illuminated manuscripts. However, monks had pattern books of animals from which to copy, and they also copied manuscripts brought into their monasteries from far afield. In the fifth or sixth century, the earliest canon tables known, in the Rabula Gospels, which were written in northern Iraq, feature several birds, including guinea fowl, ducks, chukar partridges and peacocks.

The Saxons conquered most of Britain in the fifth and sixth centuries. In an undated late Saxon site at Thetford, a peacock bone was found, so it is possible that some birds still survived in Britain throughout this period. However, trading contacts with the Near and Far East, India and Africa, as well as continental Europe, were maintained in late Saxon times by British merchants. Importation of food, especially spices and ginger from India and Africa, date back to this period, as well as garnets from India and Ceylon. Trade with Byzantine areas centred on Constantinople was undertaken from England in the sixth and seventh centuries. Illustrations of what may be intended as

A section of the Bayeux Tapestry, sewn c. 1067–70, showing peacocks on the roof of the palace in Normandy of Duke William.

peacocks appear in manuscripts from about 700 and the Latin word *pavo* appears in an eighth-century vocabulary with the translation *pauua*.[20]

Among the earliest European illuminated Gospels, those of Lindisfarne and Kells, there are some badly drawn peacocks. In the eighth-century Book of Kells birds similar to peacocks are repeatedly depicted together with the chalice and vines indicating Christ's death. They are likely to be peacocks since the peacock was a symbol of incorruption and the Resurrection.

The Romans may have been long gone, but their feasting habits seem to have been taken up by the Normans. In France, and then after 1066 in England, the peacock appeared as the centrepiece at feasts. Evidence that they were regarded as royal birds of great value appears on the Bayeux Tapestry. Many pictures of birds were sewn in the top and bottom borders the length of the tapestry. The two birds above the enthroned William the Conqueror are peacocks.

In the Domesday Book for Essex, a man named Pecoc was listed as a burgess of Colchester in 1086. In the same county, at Coggeshall, the house of a wealthy wool merchant is called Paycock House. Originally the name Peacock may have been a nickname for a man who had a distinctive walk or who was excessively proud by nature, and fond of fine clothing. Later it was used as a personal name without these connotations.

More naturalistically painted birds appeared in manuscripts about 1000, and a Gospel book, probably made at Winchester, has unmistakeable peacocks, fairly well drawn, on a canon table. Brunsdon Yapp, an authority on birds in medieval manuscripts, says that peacocks are commoner in continental manuscripts. He looked at 32 decorated continental Books of Hours and half of them had peacocks, but they were present in only 7 out of 35 English Books of Hours.[21] Two better drawn peacocks feature in the Lovell Lectionary in the British Library, while the most natural peacock was drawn in a Sketchbook owned by Samuel Pepys, but they both date from *c*. 1400.

Francis Klingender, writing about *Animals in Art and Thought to the End of the Middle Ages*, described the source of the monks' animal models for their illuminated manuscripts, after about 1150:

> They used oriental textile patterns. The bestiary illustrators adapted 'heraldic' animal patterns which had survived the industrial arts of the Middle East since Sumerian times and which the Arabs had taken over and spread westwards after their conquest of the Sassanian empire [a Persian dynasty, AD 224–636]. In the 11th century and 12th century birds and beasts within roundels formed the stock motifs, not only of Mohammedan decorative art from Seville to Baghdad, but also of Byzantine silks, then under the influence of Persia, while in the workshops of Roger II of Sicily, set up in 1147 at Palermo, both influences were combined. It was not necessary for the bestiary illustrators to leave their monasteries to look

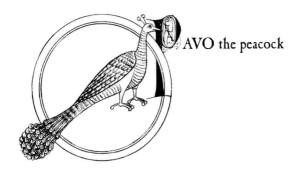

AVO the peacock

for their models, for every abbey and cathedral of note sought to enrich its treasury with just such precious eastern textiles and ivories. Even the bones of St Cuthbert were re-interred at Durham at this period wrapped in a still extant Egyptian silk of the 11th century on which appear peacocks in roundels, hunting scenes and koranic texts in Kufic script. The inventory of St Paul's Cathedral compiled in 1295 contains descriptions of many similar pieces.[22]

The Vikings were active in the ninth to eleventh centuries, operating from the Arctic to the Black Sea, thereby being able to tap the wealth of Byzantium. From Constantinople land trading routes led through Baghdad to the Persian Gulf and the silk and spice routes further east. This route may explain the presence of peacock feathers in Norway. While excavating a Viking's grave in Oslo, a small bundle of bright iridescent peacock plumes, as fresh as when put there, was discovered among his armour and weapons.

Mosaics were still being used for floor, wall and ceiling decorations, but when the peacock appears in a mosaic, it now has Christian connotations. At Venice, a series of mosaics, placed in

Noah lifting a peacock into the Ark, a detail from a 13th-century mosaic in the vestibule of St Mark's, Venice.

1215–18 in the vestibule of St Mark's on the domes and vaulted ceilings of the bays, show scenes from the Old Testament stories from the Creation until the time of Moses. One depicts Noah lifting a peacock into an ark, the peahen already inside and looking out of the doorway, while other birds wait patiently for their turn to enter the ark.

In London in 1253–4 whoever did best in the youthful game of 'Running at the Quinten' was awarded a peacock which had been prepared as a prize. In the sport of tilting, the quintain was a post for tilting at, often with a turning crosspiece to strike the unskilful tilter. The bird at this date was associated with chivalry and all the ceremony and activities of knights.

In the thirteenth century the profession of plumassier was introduced from Italy to France. Another name for it was 'chappellier de paons' or paonniers, since the trade was largely in peacock plumes. This was a flourishing trade for some time. The plumassiers formed a corporation approved by Henri III, confirmed in 1579 and again in 1593. Apprentices served four years and then produced a masterpiece before being allowed to become a master. Only members of this guild had the right to do all feather work. In England and France, early in the fourteenth century, the feather appeared for the first time as an ornament in men's hats and helmets. At first, just one long plume was used in a cap, held by a jewelled medal or in a gold brooch. By the end of the fifteenth century, feathers were used in profusion, the brims and crowns of velvet or cloth hats being closely packed with the train feathers to form very showy 'peacock's hats'. In France the plumes were worn in hunting hats, providing a crown of feathers over a hat of beaver, with a cord tied under the chin to keep it in place. A tilting helmet of this period had the same circular tightly packed crown of plumes in a metal collar above the face-guard. Hats with wide, slanted brims carried huge

Hans Burgkmair, *Maximilian I on Horseback*, 1518, woodcut. The armour was made at Innsbruck for the German emperor, 'the foremost knight of his age'. The helmet plumes are peacock feathers.

Heraldic crests of families surnamed Peacock.

lengths of peacock train feathers and were worn by the fops of the day.

Heraldry originated with single symbols used on banners and shields for recognition in battle. The insignia represented a person, family or dynasty. By the fourteenth century it had become a complex pictorial language with its own regulatory bodies (courts of chivalry) used by noble families, corporations, cities and realms. The world's oldest heraldic court is the English College of Arms, founded by Henry v (reigned 1413–22). The crests or plume of feathers on the top of helmets became separate devices to identify families, often illustrative of a surname. People called 'Peacock' adopted the bird for their heraldic crests. In Fairbairn's *Book of Crests* there are still a dozen Peacock families using images of some very decorative blue peacocks.[23]

In England, inn signs and signboards were probably adopted from the Romans who are known to have had many signs for trades including wine-sellers. Some local landowners' arms were used as signs, linking heraldry to inn signs. At Rowsley in Derbyshire, the Peacock Inn is now a fine hotel with a stone peacock on the roof over the front door. Originally built in 1652, it became the dower house of nearby Haddon Hall, the seat of the Manners family, the earls of Rutland, who had adopted a peacock for their crest.

Two great fourteenth-century English poets, William Langland (*c.* 1332–*c.* 1400) and Geoffrey Chaucer (*c.* 1345–1400), both referred to peacocks. William Langland's *Vision of William concerning Piers the Plowman* used a traditional comparison of the peacock and the lark:[24]

As for hus peyntede pennes the pocok is honoured
More than for hus faire flesh other for hus murye note . . .

Stone peacock over the front entrance to the Peacock Hotel, Rowsley, Derbyshire. The peacock appears on the family crest of the Manners family; the building, formerly their dower house, dates from 1652.

Thus the poet preiseth the pocok for hus federes,
And the riche for hus rentes othere rychesse in hus schoppe.
The lark, that is a lasse fowel, is louloker of lydene,
And swettur of sauour and swyfter of wynge.
To low-lyungemen the larke is resembled.

(The peacock is honoured for his painted feathers, rather than for his fair flesh or his merry note. Thus the poet praises the peacock for his feathers, and the rich for his rents, or riches in his trade, but the lark, that is a lesser fowl, though lovelier of voice and sweeter of taste, and swifter of wing, is likened to lowly men.)

Chaucer refers to peacocks and their feathers on several occasions. Describing a well-to-do yeoman in the Prologue to the *Canterbury Tales*, who wore a green coat and hood, and carried a sheaf of bright, sharp, peacock arrows carefully fastened under his belt, he said:

And he was clad in cote and hood of grene;
A sheefe of pecok-arrowes bright and kene
Under his belt he bar ful thriftily.

In the Reeve's Tale, the miller's character is defined 'As eny pecok he was proud and gay'. Chaucer's poem of courtly love, *Parlement of Foules*, was set in a garden with gods, lovers and birds present. The fowls are named and described, some associated with their traditional characters, for example, 'The pecock, with his aungels fethres bryght' was a phrase long used in association with the peacock. Chaucer arranged the birds in a similar order of merit as men in the feudal society of that date. First in rank were the birds of prey, then worm- and seed-eaters, lastly waterfowl. The peacock was in between the turtle-dove and pheasant, of middle rank. It is shocking to think that despite its brilliant plumage, the peacock was regarded as just another inhabitant of the barnyard. It cannot even remotely challenge the supreme position of the eagle as king of the bird-world.[25]

The use of peacock feathers for controlling the flight of arrows is first mentioned in the fourteenth century. Both the Flemings and the English made good use of peacock feathers for fletching their arrows. The feathers needed to be stiff, so it was the wing feathers of the peacock that were used. These red-brown pinions are strong and thick, although they are also brittle, which is why stronger goose quills came to be preferred. In the Wardrobe Accounts of Edward II, in 1311, is the entry 'Pro duodecim flecchis cum pennis de pavonae emptis pro rege, de 12 den' (To twelve arrows with peacock's feathers, bought for the king, 12 pence).

There were few opportunities for artists who worked under the patronage of clerics to paint birds. They were allowed to paint only biblical scenes and biblical possibilities were limited

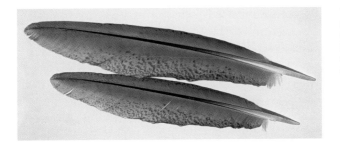

The cinnamon-coloured wing feathers of the blue peacock were once used to fletch arrows.

to the *Creation*, *Adam naming the Animals*, and the *Entry into the Ark*. These were used with enthusiasm by some of the manuscript illuminators. The artist of the East Anglian Holkham Bible filled the sky above a majestic Creator with a great cloud of birds, including an owl, peacock, jays, magpies, parrots and a hawk that was stooping on a duck, though that was hardly an episode suitable for a creation scene. These recognizable species are a great improvement on earlier manuscript pictures of birds.

The late fourteenth-century Sketchbook once owned by the diarist Samuel Pepys (now at Magdalen College, Cambridge, in the Pepysian collection), probably Italian, included lots of birds, painted in their natural colours, some quite life-like. A few labels were attached, including 'pokcoc'. This Pepysian peacock is interesting in showing the tail of the bird in correct alignment with the train and wing feathers.

During the fourteenth century many church choirs were fitted with oak seats and decorated with misericords. Several of these carvings under the seats are crisply cut wooden sculptures of peacocks, usually displaying. In the bestiaries of the time, moralists used the peacock flaunting its train to warn against the sin of pride. This may account for the misericord peacocks displaying at New College Chapel, Oxford, Wells Cathedral,

Durham Cathedral and the Priory, Cartmel. A peacock standing with train carried at rest is on a Hodnet seat. Other carved ecclesiastical peacocks of this period may be spotted on a church cornice at Adderbury, Oxfordshire, on a door at Malmesbury, Wiltshire, on stalls and benches at Bristol and Nantwich, and on a bench-end in Stogursey church, Somerset.[26]

At the coronation feast of Henry IV, in 1399, the first course consisted of cygnets, fat capons, pheasants and herons, followed by peacocks, cranes and bitterns, then a third course of aigrettes, curlews, partridges, pigeons, quails, snipe and small birds. A similar diversity of birds was served up at the installation of the Bishop of Wells, John Stafford, in 1425. Recipes of the time are specific about the peacock's preparation and presentation:

> Take a peacock, break his neck, and cut his throat. And flay him, the skin and the feathers together, and the head still to the skin of the neck. And keep the skin and the feathers whole together. Draw him as a hen, and keep the bone to the neck whole, and roast him, and set the bone of the neck above the broach [spit], as he was wont to sit alive, and above the legs to the body, as he was wont to sit alive. And when he is roasted enough, take him off and let him cool. And then wind the skin with the feathers and the tail about the body and serve him forth as he were alive, or else pull him dry, and roast him, and serve him as thou dost a hen.[27]

The peacock, again dressed in its glittering plumage, was ceremoniously carried to the table towards the end of the feast. This honour befell a lady distinguished by birth, rank or beauty, followed by a procession of ladies marching to music, who placed it before the master of the feast. There is a brass for Robert

Braunche in St Margaret's church, King's Lynn, showing a lady carrying a peacock into a feast, and an illuminated manuscript in the Morgan Library in New York has a similar scene.

If the feast followed a tournament, the knight who had won carried in the peacock and carved it. Depending on how much wine and ale had been drunk, there might follow a series of oaths taken 'on the peacock'. Placing his hand on the bird, a knight swore an oath to perform some daring deed, such as planting his standard on the walls of a besieged city, or defending his lady's honour, or anything that might occur to him, and he would probably regret the next day when sober again. This practice was referred to so frequently in the literature of the time that it seems to have been quite common in the fourteenth and fifteenth centuries.

In France, peacocks continued to be served at feasts, but a change had occurred by the time of François I (1494–1547). Now it was the custom to serve up the peacock at nobles' feasts, not to be eaten, but only to be seen. The bird had been skinned, the flesh liberally spiced, then re-covered with the skin. One bird thus preserved provided many years' extravagant display. An added excitement, especially for weddings, was provided when the bird's beak and throat were filled with cotton soaked in camphor, then set alight just before serving.

In 1420 a *Boke of Nurture* by John Russell, steward to the Duke of Gloucester, noted that in England the peacock was prepared for a feast by flaying, parboiling, larding, then sticking with cloves, before roasting it with the feet wrapped up to keep them from scorching. When cooked, the bird was covered with its skin again and underpropped so that it appeared to be standing up as when alive. Like this it was presented as a 'pecock in hakille ryally'.[28]

In London, in the 1420s, there were two brewhouses named Peahen. One was 'Pohenne without Aldgate', the other 'Pehenne yn Byshopsgatestrete'. It is curious that the recorded signs of 'Peahen' occur before any for 'Peacocks' in London, although there may have been signs unrecorded in London prior to the 1420s, or elsewhere in England. In the 1500s two more London inns with peafowl names were recorded, a 'Peyhen' in 1519 and the first 'Peacock' near the Angel in Clerkenwell Parish in 1564. The 'Peacock' was still there in the 1860s in what was then called Peacock High Street, Islington.[29]

The Italian artist Pisanello (*c.* 1395–1455) made fastidious and enchanting drawings of birds and hunting scenes with a keen eye for natural detail. Peacocks were included in his *Annunciation* (now in Venice, Accademia), *Archangel Gabriel* at Padua, and the *Vision of St Eustace* in the National Gallery, London. By the end of the 1400s, the great Renaissance artists of Italy and Northern Europe were beginning to paint in oils, mainly on panels of wood. Some of them followed the tradition of providing angels in their paintings with birds' feathers for wings. Wings composed of peacock train plumes may be seen in Netherlandish artist Hans Memling's triptych of 1473 of the *Last Judgement* (now in Gdansk). On the left section of the triptych some angels have peacock feathers with ocelli in their wings. In the central panel, the Archangel Michael stands centre-stage, weighing the souls of the dead. The warrior angel has his armour on, and over the armour a pair of large wings, the trailing ends of which are clearly eyed peacock train plumes. Memling was a pupil of Roger van der Weyden, whose similar central panel of a *Last Judgement* was unveiled at Beaune in 1451, also showing Michael wearing a pair of peacock train plume wings. In Florence, the Italian artist Francesco Botticini, about 1470, painted *Tobias and Three Archangels* in tempera on panel (Uffizi, Florence). The two outer angels have plain green and red feather wings respectively, but the

archangel holding Tobias by the hand has peacock wings.

A peacock was painted in Raphael's *Creation of the Animals*, in both Cranach's and Antonella da Messina's pictures of *St Jerome in his Study*, and Carlo Crivelli included a peacock signifying the resurrection in his *Annunciation with St Emidius*, now in the National Gallery, London.

Late in the fifteenth century, peacocks appeared on Italian maiolica made at Faenza, probably as a compliment to Cassandra Pavone (Italian for peacock), who was the mistress of Galcotto Manfredo, Lord of Faenza, and peacocks, which graced the Visconti Park in Pavia, feature in the *Visconti Hours*, now conserved in the National Library at Florence.

Among the last illuminated manuscripts produced in the Netherlands and Belgium, in the late fifteenth century, are several pictures of elaborate gardens with hedges and trees, lawns and flowerbeds, where peacocks are roaming freely and people are seated enjoying the scene.

The flow of wonderful Renaissance paintings continued into the early 1500s, notably those by the Italians Tintoretto (1518–1594) and the Bassano family, Jacopo and his son Leandro. Tintoretto delighted in painting classical subjects, including the *Origin of the Milky Way* (National Gallery, London), where Juno is clearly indicated by the presence of her peacock. Another peacock appeared in his *Lazarus and Dives*, now in Vienna, as a reference to the well-clad rich man.

In the 1500s the production of illuminated manuscripts, the bestiaries, psalters, canon tables and books of hours, ceased. With the advent of printing from woodblocks, the era of the illustrated natural history books was about to replace manuscripts. Three books about the natural history of birds, all illustrated, were published in the 1500s, *L'Histoire de la nature des oyseaux*, by the Frenchman Pierre Belon in 1555; *Historiae animalium*, by the Swiss Conrad Gesner in the years 1551–8; and *Ornithologiae hoc est de avibus historiae* by the Italian Ulisse Aldrovandi in the years 1599–1603. Belon's history of birds had 144 woodcuts, and although he looked back to the classical authors, particularly to Aristotle, he attempted to sort the birds into a classification based on his study of anatomy. His blue peacock is shown displaying. Gesner was the first author to write a comprehensive account of all known animals with references to classical sources, medieval authors and contemporary records, but arranged in alphabetical order. In the three volumes of his *Historiae animalium* there are 222 bold woodcuts of birds, some from earlier sources, others designed for this title to accompany the Latin text. Gesner anticipated that the woodcuts would appeal to 'all art lovers, doctors, painters, goldsmiths, sculptors . . . silk-embroiderers, hunters and cooks, not merely for agreeable diversion, but for practical and serviceable use'. In other words, it would act as a pattern book of designs. Gesner's book was extremely popular, being reissued several times. Aldrovandi was able to add to the information in Belon and Gesner by making a large collection of skins and paintings from which his artists and woodcutters made figures with bold outlines, and the three pictures of peacocks are among the best of the 685 illustrations in the three volumes of his *Ornithologiae*. All three authors had included similar pictures of the blue peacock, the male displaying with the head turned to the right. Aldrovandi also depicted green peacocks for the first time.

From 1560 to 1610 a feather fan was de rigeur to complete a lady's toilette. The peacock feathers with ocelli were favoured. These important accessories had ivory handles and were in general use. It was not until oriental folding fans were first introduced into Europe in Spain, late in the seventeenth century, that the feather fans were less favoured.

That the Spaniards were familiar with peacocks in the sixteenth century is in evidence in the pavane, a stately, slow dance whose name is a derivative of the Spanish *pavo* 'peacock'. It became popular in the rest of Europe over the sixteenth and

Ordo quintus.

LATINE Pauo.
ITALICE Pauon, Pauone, Pagone.
GALLICE Paon.
GERMAN. pfaw. Saxonicè Pagelûn.

A modern inn sign in St Albans, Hertfordshire, bearing a peahen, with older heraldic flourishes.

seventeenth centuries. The music for it, in 4/4 time, was designed for the careful placement of the feet of the dancers, like a peacock strutting. The performers made a wheel before each other, like that of a peacock's train, also imitating the manner in which two rival peacocks circle one another.

Apart from these few examples of peacocks in literature and art, there is little other evidence of an interest in peacocks in the sixteenth century. Since the Renaissance there had been a flourishing trade in ostrich feathers and for decorative purposes the ostrich supplanted the peacock. Although men continued to wear feathers in their hats until the end of the reign of James II (1689), they were not used in the millinery trade in Britain during the following century.

In 1570 the turkey was introduced into Britain and supplanted the peacock at feasts. Turkeys must have seemed wonderfully

Blue peacock displaying in a hand-coloured engraving from Conrad Gesner's *Historiae animalium* (Zürich, 1555). Belon's illustration has an identical pose, but in reverse.

A peasant boy wearing a peacock plume in his hat in a detail from Pieter Brueghel's oil painting *Peasant Wedding*, c. 1567.

tasty and meaty birds in comparison with the tough peacock. The peacock now became an ornamental resident of the growing number of country estates, to grace the gardens, and some were emancipated from the barnyard around this time.

John Ray's and Francis Willughby's book *Ornithologia libri tres* was published in London in 1676. 'Our main design was to illustrate the History of Birds', Ray wrote in the preface to the first illustrated systematic treatise on birds published in Britain, which formed the foundation of British ornithology. Their *Ornithologia* included two uncoloured engravings of blue peacocks. Francis Barlow (c. 1626–1704) painted fish and fowl, and etched prints of them, at the same time John Ray was publishing. Barlow's paintings were much more realistic, though both he and Ray's workmen had live models in Charles II's collection of birds in St James's Park from which to draw. Barlow's picture of a cassowary, pheasant, ostrich, peacock and peahen was probably compiled from sketches made in the king's aviaries. Barlow placed the peacocks in an exotic setting, like many of the paintings by Dutch artists of the seventeenth century.

TAB.XXVII

Pavo The Peacock.

Engravings of 'Pavo The Peacock' standing and displaying, from John Ray and Francis Willughby's *Ornithologia libri tres* (1676).

About 1639 Rembrandt painted one of the most remarkable pictures of a peacock ever put on canvas. Rarely did Rembrandt paint birds and his *Still Life with Two Dead Peacocks and a Girl, c.* 1639, is a tour de force in the painting of feathers. It is not known where he obtained the bird (probably the same specimen painted twice) or why he chose to paint it as a still-life subject. Other Dutch and Flemish artists painted still-life pictures of birds at a slightly later date. The Dutch artist Melchior d'Hondecoeter (1636–1695) was the best bird painter of the

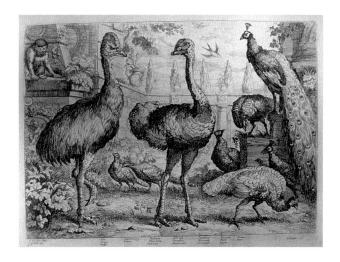

An etching by Francis Barlow from his *Birds and Fowles* (1665). Barlow was the first English artist to place the peacock in a garden setting.

Golden Age of Dutch and Flemish Art. Several of his large oil paintings feature the gardens of country seats with a mixture of lively barnyard fowl and exotic foreign bird species. The birds are well observed, active and beautifully painted. They reflected the taste of well-travelled wealthy gentlemen, who could afford to keep bird collections on their estates. Peacocks took pride of place in these paintings, usually standing high on plinths or urns so that their trains flowed gracefully down to the ground and could be painted in all their glory.

A London 'Peacock Brewhouse in White Cross Street' Cripplegate, *c.* 1648–72, was but one of a score of London peacock sign names of the seventeenth century. One Peacock Inn owner was more enterprising, adding an epigram to the sign in 1636:

Though Argus eyes be in the Peacocks taile,
A man may drinke there till his eye-sight faile;

But if a man a good Decorum keepe,
Hee'l see the clearer and more soundly sleepe.

Sign boards with pictures of peacocks were not only hung in the
street to advertise taverns but were used by hosiers, booksellers,
boot and shoe makers and linen drapers as well as breweries.[30]

In the eighteenth century chefs both in Holland and in
England were seized with a brief, nostalgic urge to make peacock
pies again. The cook to the Duke of Bolton, John Nott, wrote
The Cook's and Confectioner's Dictionary, published in 1723. It
had two peacock recipes, one 'To boil a peacock' and the second
'To bake a peacock in a pye'. The first recipe cunningly minced
the peacock flesh into such small pieces before adding so many
other ingredients that it would have been difficult to identify
the peacock meat when it had been boiled.

45. To boil a Peacock.

FLEY off the Skin, but leave the Rump whole with the Pinions, then mince the Flesh raw with some Beef-suet, season with Salt, Pepper, Nutmeg, and savoury Herbs shred small, and Yolks of Eggs raw; mingle with these some Marrow, the Bottoms of three Artichokes boil'd, Chesnuts roasted and blanch'd, and Skirrets boil'd pretty small; then fill the Skin of the Peacock, and prick it up in the Back, set it to stew in a deep Dish in some strong Broth, White-wine, with Salt, large Mace, Marrow, Artichokes boil'd and quarter'd, Chesnuts, Grapes, Barberries, Pears quarter'd, and some of the Meat made into Balls, cover it with another large Dish; when it is stew'd enough, serve it up on carv'd Sippets, broth it, and garnish with slices of Lemon, and Lemon-peel whole, run it over with beaten Butter, garnish the Dish with the Yolks of hard Eggs, Chesnuts, and large Mace.

46. To bake a Peacock in a Pye.

BONE your Peacock, parboil it, and lard it with large Lardons of Bacon; then season it with Salt, Pepper and Nutmeg, of each two Ounces and a half; when your Pye is ready, lay some Butter in the Bottom, with some Cloves beaten; then lay in your Peacock, and the rest of the seasoning upon it, lay good store of Butter, close it, baste it with Saffron-water, and when it is bak'd and cold, fill it with clarified Butter.

In the first half of the eighteenth century two bird artists were at work in Britain painting brightly coloured canvases in oils, full of lively birds in spacious landscapes. One artist was English, Marmaduke Cradock (1660–1717), the other was from Antwerp but spent most of his life in England, Pieter Casteels (1684–1749). Both were working for patrons with large country estates. The paintings were reminders for their owners of their Grand Tours of Europe. An artist needed a royal or aristocratic patron, with a menagerie of exotic species, in order to paint can-

vases alive with colourful foreign species of birds. Jakob
Bogdani (1660–1724) had access to parrots and colourful waterfowl when he painted in Admiral George Churchill's menagerie.
An example of Bogdani's work concentrates on blue peafowl
and includes a white and a pied variety of the species. The paintings were factual, sober records of what peacocks looked like,
without any moralistic or religious overtones, for eighteenth-
century art was free of overlaid symbolism. Nevertheless, the
old prejudices against peacocks persisted, as William Cowper

reminded his readers when he took an amused look at the bird in his poem *Truth* (1781, 1. 58):

The self-applauding bird, the peacock see –
Mark what a sumptuous Pharisee is he.

This prejudice had been exported to America by the Pilgrim Fathers. It surfaced, unexpectedly, when George Washington, wrote down some *Rules of Civility* in 1754. Rule 54 states: 'Play not the Peacock, looking everywhere about you, to see if you be well deck't.' A painting by Junius Brutus Stearns of *Washington and the Indians* (painted 1847) showed Washington on a mission to the leaders of the Iroquois confederacy at Logstown, on the Ohio River, in 1753. One of the Indian women is wearing a feathered cape in which peacock train feathers have been incorporated. American researchers have found that peacock feathers were traded occasionally in the 1830s to the Indian Sauk and Mesquakies.[31] As so often, the feathers preceded the live birds in the peacock's extension of its presence westwards.

The king who lost the American colonies had a very curious, fleeting association with the peacock. As he was recovering from one of his bouts of illness, his ministers decided that George III was fit enough to make a speech. The king was inclined to gabble at high speed, so, in order to slow him down, even if they could not make him articulate clearly, they suggested that he whisper the word 'peacock' at the end of every sentence. It did indeed slow him down, but what sense the audience made of it is not recorded, or why the ministers chose the word 'peacock'.

In the 1780s in France and England there was a revival of the fashion for wearing peacock feathers in hats, but with a difference. This time, the feathers decorated women's, not men's,

Detail of an elaborate fan with peacock plumes in Ingres' oil painting *La Grande Odalisque*, 1814.

hats. Marie Antoinette led this fashion, by placing peacock and ostrich feathers in her coiffure one evening. It was commented upon favourably by her husband, Louis XVI, and so the new fashion was born. The French example was quickly emulated by other European courts and the demand for peacock and ostrich feathers soared. After this, the wearing of peacock and other feather-decorated hats persisted as a ladies' fashion until the end of the reign of George V in Britain, about 1936. A further use for peacock feathers in eighteenth-century Europe was an amateur pastime of making panels of feather work for hangings, and realistic pictures of birds to hang on the wall.

Richard Bowlker, in *The Art of Angling* (1774) first mentioned the Peacock Fly for salmon fishermen by name, so-called because it was designed to have the wing of the salmon fly made from the neck or train feathers taken from a peacock. The peacock herl (several barbs) was cut from the green strands of the ornate train feathers, and several variants on this design have been used ever since. The soft feathery quality and the sparkling glint of the peacock feather give the fly a natural appearance. A variant is the Black and Peacock Spider, a traditional trout wet fly good on any still water or, in smaller sizes, on faster flowing rivers. Peafowl feathers are still extensively used today in fishing for making trout and salmon flies. The herl is used to construct the body or thorax of the artificial flies. Quills of peacock feathers are also used to make floats for coarse fishing.

By the end of the nineteenth century there had long been a campaign to ban the use of feathers in millinery. The campaign denounced the wearing of birds' plumage because so many birds, egrets in particular, were killed in order to satisfy the immense demand. The protests came from both sides of the Atlantic. In the American bird magazine *The Auk*, a list of one London firm's sales was published, which included '16,000 packages and bundles of osprey, peacock, argus and other pheasants, etc and several thousand *mats* and *handscreens*'. The report continued: 'Last year the trade in birds for women's hats was so enormous that a single London dealer admitted that he had sold 2,000,000 of small birds of every kind and color.'[32] Charles Beebe underlined this, writing from experience of the Indian end of this peacock feather trade, about 1920:

Until recently the traffic in their skins and trains was enormous. 70,000 bundles of eyed plumes have been imported by one dealer in England in a single week. Most of the plumes gathered in India are exported although on the South West coast there is an industry of considerable size, the feathers being used to decorate hand-screens, fans and mats made of kaskas grass.[33]

The National Audubon Society of America was founded in 1886 and the Society for the Protection of Birds in Britain in 1891, largely spurred on by a determination to stop this trade. Legislation banning these excessive imports took decades to achieve. The natural moult and casting of the train would account for some of the peacock plumes, but not all. During and after the Second World War, bans on importation of unnecessary goods hastened the end of the trade in all kinds of feathers. Archery was revived in England, as a sport in 1844, but this put little pressure on the peacock feather trade.

The interest in peacocks had been intense while they were novelties and being spread to the west. This interest dwindled considerably between 1600 and the next intense period, which occurred at the end of the nineteenth century. This was the time when craftsmen of the Arts and Crafts Movement, Aesthetic Movement and Art Nouveau adopted the peacock in their designs. Throughout these centuries, when the peacock was constantly being caged and sent on long journeys to the west, once at its destination it was kept in captivity or semi-domesticated, rarely colonizing or naturalizing its new territory. Very few feral populations succeeded in establishing themselves and leading independent lives. Any birds found roaming freely were snared, killed and eaten, probably by people aggravated beyond endurance by the birds' harsh cries and destructive habits in gardens. Attempts to maintain a beautiful garden invariably fail if an owner introduces even a small muster of blue peacocks. Not for nothing has the bird earned the reputation of having the feathers of an angel, the voice of the devil and feet of which it is thoroughly ashamed.

There are billions of domestic fowl on the earth today, all of them descended from the species *Gallus gallus*, or similar jungle fowls of eastern Asia. They were distributed at the same time, through the same routes as the blue peacock, to the same areas, from northern India. Domestic fowl have been produced in a huge variety of forms, as a result of centuries of cross-breeding for meat, eggs or fancy plumage. For 3,000 years the blue peafowl was also steadily distributed further to the west from India and Sri Lanka, but it has retained its specific integrity and never been fully domesticated. What we see today when admiring blue peafowl is almost certainly what Solomon saw and prized so highly.

Thomas Bewick's wood-engraved vignette of a fashionable woman wearing a peacock plume in her hat.

5 The Green Peacock
in the East

All authors writing about the green peacock, *Pavo muticus*, agree that it is far more delicate than the blue species, breeds less readily and is much shyer, avoiding human habitation even where protected. Many also comment on the poor choice of name for the species by Linnaeus in 1766, for the bird could not remotely be called mute or silent, its voice being only slightly less strident than that of the blue peacock. Although similar physically to the blue peacock, the green is very different in character. The blue is sociable, living in a muster of fourteen to fifteen birds and even larger groups; the green is found only with three or four family members. The blue leaves the forests and associates with people in their villages and may be found in large numbers around Hindu temples. The green peacock lives deep in the jungle and is intolerant of people. Blue male peacocks live together peaceably, and although they spar with each other in the breeding season, they do not kill another blue peacock in a fight, nor will they kill smaller birds. The green peacock will fight another male to the death and will attack and kill smaller birds, and even attack people. It would be relatively safe for a child to stray near a blue peacock, but a wise parent would keep it well away from a green peacock. This unsociable behaviour means that the green peacock is not often seen even in its native haunts, little is known of it and very little written about it. The

Burmese did not domesticate wild animals and they and other peoples sharing localities with green peacocks did not attempt to domesticate them. Where green peacocks are in aviaries in the west, the males are kept separately, which is why so few green peafowl are to be seen in Europe or America.

The distribution of the indigenous green peacock is far-flung, and the birds are now sparse within each location. There are three races or subspecies of green peafowl, living in clearly defined, separate areas, called the Javan, Indo-Chinese and Burmese Green Peacock. The first two differ only in the intensity of their green colouration, and some other small features, but the Burmese bird's plumage is bluer and duller and there is more black and less gold in the back.

The range for the Javan green peafowl *Pavo muticus muticus* is confined to Java now, though it once was found in Thailand and the Malay Peninsula. In Java it is protected by law but this does not prevent its being heavily hunted both for its meat and train feathers. The feathers are used in local dances. That the subspecies could have lost so much terrain and now largely be restricted to the small island of Java is both disheartening and alarming.

The Javanese believe firmly in the intimacy between tigers and peacocks, saying that the peacock likes to feed on the intestinal worms of the tiger's victims after the tiger has left its prey. In both Java and Burma there is a widespread belief that it is very dangerous to have a peacock near young children because the birds are fond of swallowing precious stones and are deceived by the eyes of children and endeavour to peck them out.[1] The peacock does not figure largely in Javan art, which is mainly concerned with images of the Buddha. An incense burner or bronze figure in the shape of a peacock may be found in some temples, but the peacock is not closely associated there with the Buddha in any form.

When the green peacock was present in Malaya, it was called *Merak*, an onomatopoeic name. This described the harsh call, but the bird has a second call, subdued although still penetrating, a cry of several syllables. In Malay states the peacock was considered an unclean bird and not eaten by Muslims. They believed that it guided the serpent to the Tree of Knowledge in the Garden of Eden and hence it is under an eternal curse. Malays of other faiths readily ate the flesh – that of young birds being considered delicious, though the adult cocks were known to be unbelievably tough.[2]

The Indo-Chinese green peafowl was named *Pavo muticus imperator* in 1949, by a Frenchman, Jean Delacour (1890–1985), who led seven expeditions to Indo-China (now Vietnam, Laos and Cambodia) between the world wars, collecting bird skins and living specimens, some new to science. He recognized that the Indo-Chinese peafowl varied sufficiently in colour from the Javanese and Burmese green peafowl to warrant its being made a separate subspecies of *Pavo muticus*.[3] The subspecies was previously distributed in eastern Burma, the extreme south of Yunnan, in Thailand, in Laos and in Vietnam. It is becoming increasingly rare in Vietnam, however, and the only viable population left in Thailand is protected in the Huai Kha Wildlife Sanctuary. Much work has been done in the past few years in Thailand to try to save its last main habitat and in importing wild birds. In Indonesia the World Pheasant Association has funded a pilot study to find the best conditions for its conservation.[4]

The best place to observe peacocks in Thai art is in one of their Theravada Buddhist temples or wats. A remarkable wood carving of a peacock was made for the eaves of the Teal Library in the compound of Wat Phra That Haripunchai in Lamphun, an ancient town in northern Thailand. Another, on a gable

A painting by Araki Kampo (1831–1915) of a green peacock in a hurry.

board over the entrance to Wat Phan To in Chiang Mai, is obviously inspired by Burmese art and is a common motif in temple decorations, where the peacock represents the Burmese sunbird. With abundant forests all over Thailand, architectural

wood-carving emerged as a major craft early in the kingdom of
Siam's history. Thai temples are mostly roofed with timber, giving ample scope for the wood-carver to create favourite figures,
both human and mythological.[5] Among the Hindu gods in Thai
art, Skandakumara, a war god with twelve arms, is shown riding on a green peacock. He is similar to Karittekya, the war god
of India, who rides on a blue peacock.

The peacock's feathers were particularly treasured for head-
dresses, and the men of South Vietnam still wear peacock feathers
in their hair. The Vietnamese regard peacocks as symbols of peace
and prosperity. The bird itself is increasingly rare in Vietnam
owing to habitat loss, but it now has national protection status.[6]

The plight of the Burmese green peafowl is even worse. *Pavo
muticus spicifer*, named by Shaw and Nodder in 1804, was formerly found in Assam, north-east India, south through

A carved wooden peacock on the gable-board of Wat Phan To, Chiang Mai, Thailand.

Manipur and the Chittagong and Lushai Hills of Bangladesh, and also in western Myanmar and east to the Irrawaddy River. It is now extinct through much of this range. Recent information suggests that it clings on in Assam, and parts of western Burma, but the Burmese green peafowl may, in truth, no longer be found in Burma. As in the other regions, habitat loss and pot-hunting are blamed for the decline. Early evidence of trading in peacock feathers exists from Burma in the eighth century AD, when the Mekong River was used as a highway to the north.

A new dynasty was established in Burma in 1752, Konbaung, with a peacock as its insignia. The royal boats, gilded war canoes manned by 40 to 60 men using gilded oars, carried a flag with the Kon-baung peacock emblem. The throne and furniture in the Royal Hall of Audience had symbolic peacocks and rabbits as decoration, representing the sun and moon. Elsewhere the emblem is a prevalent motif over entrances to buildings, especially those built during this period, 1752–1885. While the British were in Burma, from 1886 to 1948, the nation's flag bore a small picture of a displaying peacock. During the colonial period shell-carving was noted as a flourishing by-product of Burma's pearl-fishing industry. Images such as peacocks, people and landscapes may be found either painted, carved or etched into the shells using traditional Burmese designs.

Old traditions linger on. Today, the birds may be vanishing but there is a flourishing trade in papercrafts where they are remembered. Though mainly produced for the tourist market, the Burmese also enjoy a form of origami and treat it more seriously. On special occasions, as an act of merit, a donor may commission objects in the shape of a peacock and flowers, among other natural subjects, for presentation to a pagoda or monastery where they are offered to the gods. It is to be hoped that the gods protect the tiny lingering population of the real green peacocks, if any remain.

The green peacock has long been famous in China and Japan where it was imported from Indo-China, Malaya and Java, from all over the former range of the three subspecies. Most of the eastern art inspired by the bird, which we know in the west, is Chinese or Japanese in origin. We became familiar with paintings and prints depicting peacocks with flowers and in landscapes when they were imported in the nineteenth century. These are pictures of the green peacock, though most people in the west assume the bird to be the blue peacock.

Green peacocks of the subspecies *Pavo muticus imperator* are indigenous in a number of sites in Yunnan at the border with Burma and Laos, but the population is declining. At Jinghong, a Chinese town on the borders of Burma and Laos, there are open markets where green peacock feather fans can be purchased. The feathers come from the peacocks inhabiting the Jinghong forests. Xishuang Banna, a semi-tropical prefecture in the south of China near the borders with Laos and Myanmar, is known in China as the 'home of the peacock'. Visitors there can buy peacock train feathers, which, one hopes, are dropped naturally. Programmes of rearing captive peacocks are currently under way in Longling county in west Yunnan province, and other peacocks are being preserved in land set aside in forest

Anonymous Northern Song Dynasty (AD 960–1127), *Winter Plum and Peacock*, colour on silk.

Cui Bai (Northern
Song Dynasty,
AD 960–1127),
*Peacock and
Fruit Tree*,
colour on silk.

near Qinghua in the Dali Bai autonomous prefecture and in the capital Kunming's zoological garden.

We may think of the green peacock as a Chinese bird, but it occurs only in Yunnan, and Yunnan was not Chinese until it was over-run by Kublai Khan's Mongol hordes in 1253 and assimilated into his empire. Before 1253, however, the peacock, blue or green or both, was known to the Chinese and was kept in captivity. In the Tang Dynasty (AD 618–907) China traded with, and influenced, many nearby countries – Japan, Korea, Tibet, Cambodia and Burma – and opened up sea, river and land routes. China exported silk and imported luxury goods. Ships from the Indian Ocean took exotic items to Chinese cities, for example silver from Annam, now part of Vietnam, dyes from Indonesia and spices from Persia. Anything rare, beautiful and exotic was appreciated by the Chinese and peacocks certainly fall within those categories. Chinese influence on the countries where green peacocks are found in the wild explains the availability of this bird's feathers and living specimens in China for many centuries. The green peacock became a symbol of beauty and dignity and is often coupled in paintings with the tree peony, a symbol of spring, or a peony expressing love and feminine beauty.

The peacock was so familiar in China that it became incorporated into the symbolism of Chinese deities. A cult formed around the Taoist Queen Mother of the West about the end of the first millennium BC, when she was portrayed riding on a white crane, or less often on a peacock. When the crane was substituted by a peacock is not known, but perhaps after an artist had seen a peacock, or a picture of one, for the first time. Xi Wang Mu, the Queen Mother of the West, lived in a golden palace on the summit of Mount Kunlun, a mythical peak in the west. The walls of some 530 kilometres that surrounded the palace were topped with battlements of precious stones. She was served by five Jade Fairy Maids, and had a flock of bluebirds as messengers. Peaches of immortality grew in her gardens, but they took 3,000 years to grow and another 3,000 years to ripen. When one ripened, it called for a celebratory feast, and was greatly prized.[7]

The fabulous bird Fung-whang or Feng-Huang, the Chinese Phoenix on Chinese screens, owes much of its ancestry to the peacock. The Feng-Huang is not strictly a phoenix but a mixture of a stork, peacock and pheasant. In Chinese art both the dragon and the phoenix were symbols of felicity and complement each other. The phoenix decorates ceramic wares of all but the

Chinese filigree-worked pin with gems, turquoises and a gold peacock,
c. 1736–96, from the Xinglong Shanxiang imperial tomb in Kilin province, China.

earliest period. The dragon is symbol of the emperor, the phoenix of the empress.

The Chinese love fairy tales and have some charming stories in which peacocks feature as agents to provide a happy ending. One story tells how the smallest and most ordinary peacock in the forest won by his unselfishness the treasured gift of magic powers, so that his train feathers glowed until they shone brilliantly like shooting stars as he flew over towns and villages at the time of the Spring Festival. Now, every year when the Spring Festival comes the brilliant colours in the little peacock's train are to be seen flashing and dancing among the fireworks as the Chinese celebrate.[8] Another peacock assisted Sea Girl, daughter of the Dragon King, to find the golden key to release the waters of a great lake so that the fields of her parched village might be watered.[9]

The peacock feather is an attribute of Kwan-Yin, the goddess of mercy. Feathers were highly valued by the emperor and his subjects. In the Summer Palace Hall of Benevolence and Longevity in Beijing, beside the sandalwood throne carved with nine dragons, two tall columns support large bowls in which a great number of peacock train feathers were put to create a regal atmosphere. That this was a long-standing tradition over a wide area in the east can be deduced from early paintings of assemblies and courts that show vases of peacock feathers flanking the throne of the Mughals in India, among other potentates.

The eyed feathers were granted as a reward of merit to mandarins. Chinese emperors from the Ming Dynasty (1368–1644) onwards bestowed the train feathers on those they wished to honour. Beebe stated: 'In spite of the wide-spread notion, these indicate neither office nor rank, the nine grades of mandarins being distinguished by the colour of the buttons on their caps.'[10] However, the peacock was used as one insignia of rank

on badges among the emperor's civil servants. Rank badges, usually 27.5 centimetres square, were sewn onto the back and front of a servant of the emperor's formal gown. Military ranks wore badges depicting mammals; civil ranks wore badges depicting birds, the first rank being a crane, second rank a golden pheasant and the third rank a peacock.

Fine Chinese porcelain has been admired since it was first imported to Europe in the seventeenth century. Porcelain kilns in southern China, in Jianxi province around the town of Jingdezhen, produced great quantities of quality porcelain, especially during the early years of the Qing Dynasty (1644–1911). The greatest period of Chinese ceramics, in the reign of Emperor Kangxi (1662–1722) was the result of their mastery of kiln technology, refined clays and the skilled use of deep cobalt-blue for decoration. The cobalt provided a brilliant contrast against the

A 19th-century painting of an imperial Chinese audience at which all officials performed the kowtow to the emperor as a symbol of their submission to his will. Each official wore a peacock feather and a ruby button in his hat.

A Chinese civil servant's badge for the third rank, 'Peacock'.

A Chinese court official's hat, with ruby button and peacock feather.

A glazed porcelain dish of the Kangxi period (1662–1722) decorated with peacocks.

perfect foil of the pure white, smooth and translucent body. The effect is stunning, as in a large dish of the Kanxi period, made *c.* 1710–12, decorated with peacocks and flowers, which is a superb example of the Chinese potters' work.

In the late nineteenth century an empress dowager rebuilt the emperors' Summer Palace. The Hall of Benevolent Longevity was rebuilt in 1890, with an elaborate red sandalwood Peacock Throne flanked by two big fans of peacock feathers. Tz'u-hsi (or Ci Xi) spent lavishly on buildings and had several elaborate jewelled thrones, the cost of which contributed to the impoverishment of her country. She frequently had her portrait painted, seated on one of her thrones, especially in her sixtieth year, when

Ci Xi, dowager empress of China, on the Peacock Throne.

the hem of her state dress was embroidered with the symbols of longevity.

Centuries after blue peacocks had been familiar birds strutting round the barnyards and gardens of western Europe, the green peafowl was still unknown in the west. Ironically, the first indication that a green peacock existed came from the one major country in the Far East where the green peacock was not indigenous, Japan. The Italian author Ulisse Aldrovandi included wood engravings of a male and a female green peacock in the second volume of his book *Ornithologiae*, issued in 1600. The illustrations were copied from drawings of the birds sent to Innocent IX (pope only from October to December 1591) by the Emperor of Japan, among other birds 'drawn from the life'. Aldrovandi said they had been sent to Italy by ' D. Caesar Facchinetto, Marquis and Senator for our town,' who was also an ambassador to Japan. The engraving of the male bird captured the unique facial markings, the tufted crest and long legs, to which was added a picture of a locust. He also included an engraving of the female, like the male except with no long train, but accompanied by an ear of wheat. It seems clear that he thought the crest of the green peafowl (both male and female) had the same shape and size as an ear of corn. (This inference was used in 1804 by Shaw and Nodder when they called the green peafowl 'Spiked peafowl, Pavo spicifer', *spica* being Latin for an ear of wheat.) Still having no specimens of their own from which to illustrate this bird, the French ornithologists Brisson, in 1760, and Buffon, in 1770–86, copied Aldrovandi's woodcuts, and Linnaeus named the bird from the drawing *Pavo muticus* in 1766.[11]

Woodcuts after drawings sent to Rome from Japan of a male green peacock with locust and a female peacock with an ear of wheat, from Ulisse Aldrovandus's *Ornithologia* (1600).

In England, John Latham used a specimen (a skin) when he included it in *A General Synopsis of Birds* (1781–5). As for other specimens of the green peacock, the Dutch ornithologist Conraad Jacob Temminck in 1813 said that no specimen had found its way into European museums, but a Frenchman, François Levaillant, had seen some living in an aviary in Cape Town, sent from Macao.[12] There is no accurate information about the living birds being imported into Europe before Edward T. Bennet mentioned two living specimens in the London Zoo in 1831, sent from Burma by Lord Holmesdale. Live green peafowl were later imported into Europe and bred in Holland some time before 1872 and in France by 1873.

The scholarly authority on Japanese art, George Ashdown Audsley, wrote in 1882:

Representations of the peacock are great favourites with the Japanese artists, and they are successfully given in nearly all branches of their decorative arts. They are cleverly rendered in their kakemono and screen paintings; on their large dishes and other articles of porcelain; and carefully modelled and cast in bronze.[13]

There is a story in connection with the arrival of the peacock in Japan, about three centuries ago. Guests of a Prince of Hizen entertained at a banquet were asked to inspect a pair of new foreign birds – peafowl. The prince asked his guests which was the male and which the female. The gentlemen, turning to the gaily dressed ladies and wishing to complement them, said the most beautiful bird must be the female. The ladies modestly decided it must be the male. 'You are right', the prince said to the ladies, 'Nature herself will have the male best clad; and it seems to me incomprehensible that the wife should have more pride and desire to go more richly dressed than her husband, who must be at the expense of maintaining her.'[14]

The peacock became sufficiently well known and popular to be grafted onto Japan's pantheon of gods and associations with the Buddha. There are several fine paintings of peacocks in the museums of Japan depicting the Buddha, for example, the Peacock-King/Buddha riding on a displaying peacock. In parts of Japan the peacock is sacred to a goddess of mercy, Kwannon. A sage riding a peacock in Japanese painting is Kujaku-Myo-O, a Buddha of healing, thought to be derived from Vairocana, one of a group of five Buddhas of Meditation.

In the eighteenth century the peacock was incorporated in Japanese embroideries, of which a polychrome figured silk sur-

18th-century Japanese embroidery with peacocks.

coat with peacock feathers (in the Victoria and Albert Museum, London) is a beautiful example. Another elaborate, rich embroidery of peacocks on deep blue satin, dusted in places with gold powder, is described by Audsley in 1882. The feathers of the cock are laid in strong twisted silk threads, those of the tail being in light brown and green silk and gold cleverly plaited together, with the eyes in floss silk. The feathers of the hen are in floss silk executed in feather stitch. To complete the picture, the eyes of both birds are applied in glass. The *fukusa* (embroidery) measures 76 by 63.5 centimetres. Another Japanese embroidery of the eighteenth century is now in the Stibbert Museum, Florence. These were costly fabrics, only for ceremonial and imperial wear.

Ogata Korin (1658–1716), Japan's greatest decorative painter, produced *Peacocks with Plum-Blossom and Hollyhocks*, (*c.* 1701–

Ogata Korin, *Peacocks with Plum-Blossom and Hollyhocks,* a male displaying to a female, on an early 18th-century Japanese folding screen.

10), probably for a wealthy patron, perhaps a member of a shogun family with whom the hollyhock was associated, who may have owned a green peacock and kept it in his garden. If Audsley is correct, and the green peacock was introduced into Japan about 1680, then this will be among the earliest Japanese paintings of the species done from a living bird. The plum, on the other hand, was long known and depicted as an attribute of the Shinto patron of poetry and the arts, Kitano Tenjin (845–903). Its blossom was welcome, appearing very early in the spring, before its leaves had appeared.

Many Japanese artists painted flowers with birds (*kacho-e*), a favourite being the peacock and peony, the bird representing beauty and dignity combined with the tree peony as a symbol of Spring. Utagawe Hiroshige (1797–1858) painted a vertical diptych (*kakemono-e*) of this combination, early in the 1840s. *Kakemono-e* wood-block prints were often displayed on the walls of Japanese houses, an inexpensive substitute for the costly scroll paintings of the wealthy. A peacock with peonies was one of Hiroshige's favourite *kacho-e* subjects. Araki Kampo (1831–1914), a minor Japanese artist, painted a very flamboyant and vigorous portrait of a green peacock, on the run, away from the observer. Its train feathers may be exaggerated, but it is delightful to see such movement in a peacock painting. A very fine Satsuma faience vase bearing a peacock and a peahen shows the artistic grace of the Japanese artist of this period (*c*. 1868–1912). It was concurrent with the Art Nouveau period in the west, which was inspired by Japanese styles. The male depicted on this vase was probably the inspiration for one of the peacocks on the south wall of Whistler's Peacock Room (see pp. 154–6).

Today, the opportunity to see green peafowl is much greater in viewing Japanese and Chinese paintings than in the chance of seeing a living bird. A few breeders now successfully rear green

Utagawa Hiroshige, *Peacock and Peonies*, woodblock print of a green peacock and a tree peony, early 1840s.

A peacock-adorned Satsuma faience vase and stand.

peacocks in Britain, where the species seems to have become better acclimatized and a little more hardy over the years. The species as a whole needs protection throughout its range if people in the future are going to be able to enjoy their beautiful plumage.

6 Artefacts and Architecture

In the east, peacocks have long been an integral part of the art serving religious faiths and cultures. As the bird was exported to the west, its decorative value was appreciated by Middle Eastern artists, potters and mosaicists. In western Europe, peacocks appeared in illuminated manuscripts in the Middle Ages. The birds were thereafter absent from European art, except for a brief period when they were incorporated in paintings of Dutch, Flemish and English country-estate gardens, where they were prestigious decorative elements, symbols of the wealth of their owners. Then, in the mid-nineteenth century, a series of events triggered an explosion of artefacts featuring peacocks that was to last for half a century. During this period, it would have been possible to have a house filled with peacocks, where they figured on fabrics, metal firescreens, fireside tiles, stained-glass windows, lamps and on wallpapers, besides ceramic and glass vases shaped like peacocks, coloured like peacocks or decorated with peacock feathers. From the evidence of contemporary paintings, even the ladies gracing these rooms were themselves decked out in peacock feathers. This last wave of peacock awareness affected the design of artefacts, rather than, as formerly, paintings.

The Great Exhibition of the Industries of all Nations held in London in 1851 made the British aware of the riches of art, archi-

A Lalique peacock car mascot from the late 1920s.

tecture and artefacts from all over the world. Each nation, in its allotted hall at the Crystal Palace, showed off its peoples, culture and the products of its country. After the exhibition, many exhibits were bought for the new South Kensington Museum (now the Victoria and Albert Museum) and became study collections for British designers. Two of them, William Morris and William de Morgan, formed a new English social and aesthetic movement called the Arts and Crafts Movement.

Edgar Maxence, *Peacock Profile*, c. 1896, pastel and gouache on paper. Maxence was a Symbolist who adopted Art Nouveau images of the period, including medieval subjects and fashions.

Morris had been at Oxford University with John Ruskin, who became of immense influence as a writer and critic and, as Slade Professor of Art at Oxford, through his lectures on art, architecture and natural history. Ruskin's idealistic views on the importance of hand-crafting and creativity for the benefit of both the artisan and consumer formed the philosophical foundation of the Arts and Crafts Movement. Ruskin was interested in the natural patterns and colours in nature, especially in birds' plumage, and made some extraordinarily sensitive and painstakingly detailed drawings of feathers, including a peacock's feather, of which he wondered how he could 'ever accomplish without having heaven to dip my brush in' (see illustration on p. 95).[1]

William Morris aimed to improve the quality of hand-crafted goods, especially fabrics, after seeing so many machine-produced artefacts of poor quality. Like Ruskin, he thought hand-made goods were superior in every way, with a beneficial effect on those who made them as well as the users. He went back before the Industrial Revolution to find inspiration for his designs, and was especially fond of the bright colours, fabrics and motifs of the Middle Ages. That had been a period when peacocks were prominent, in illuminated manuscripts, religious art and men's costume, so inevitably they featured in his designs for stained glass, wallpaper and fabrics. His interest in embroidery resulted in an association with the Royal School of Needlework, where several folding screens with peacocks from his designs were made.

William De Morgan designed this ruby lustre earthenware dish of c. 1885–92, hand-painted with a peacock in full display.

A William De Morgan multiple-tile design with peacock and lizards.

A silver, opal and mother-of-pearl Arts and Crafts peacock brooch designed by C. R. Ashbee (1863–1942).

William De Morgan was a potter who worked for Morris & Co. in the 1860s, designing stained glass and tiles. He was interested in the chemistry of glazes and discovered how to produce metallic lustre glazes similar to those produced in the twelfth to thirteenth centuries. The glazes were the perfect medium for imitating the iridescent plumage of peacocks. Much of his work was inspired by the Middle East, especially Iznik pottery made at a pottery centre in the Ottoman Empire in the sixteenth century, featuring long curling leaves and stylized flowers. De Morgan designed many tiles with peacocks, some of them for new Victorian fireplaces. Early fireplaces had been made almost entirely of metal, but in the second half of the century decoration was supplied by panels of tiles with flowers, birds and even characters from stories.

Another member of the movement, Walter Crane, a painter, designer and book illustrator, achieved fame in Britain in the 1870s as a nursery book illustrator. His *Baby's Own Aesop* (1887) contained the peacock fables and 'the Peacock complaining to Juno'. The designs in these books had a far-reaching influence, despite being originally aimed at children. Charles Robert Ashbee was a pioneer of Arts and Crafts jewellery produced on aesthetic principles. He set up the Guild and School of Handicraft in the East End of London in 1888 and designed much of its output. The choice of less valuable stones and use of enamelling rather than expensive metals made the brooches, pendants and necklaces available to those of moderate means. The value of a personal ornament was assumed to consist not in the commercial cost of the materials, so much as in the artistic quality of its design. He used stones that reflected the expanding British Empire, with opals from Australia, pearls from India, moonstones from Ceylon (Sri Lanka) and South African diamonds. However, several of his necklaces featuring peacocks were made of silver, gold, pearls and diamonds, with a ruby for the eye.

A whole room devoted to peacocks, inspired by their green-blue plumage, was designed in a house in London in 1876–7. It became known as 'The Peacock Room' when it was completed by the American artist James McNeill Whistler (1834–1903). Originally, it was the dining room of 49 Prince's Gate, the London home of Frederick Leyland, a wealthy ship owner. Whistler had lived and worked in London since 1863, and became the friend of the poet and painter Dante Gabriel Rossetti (1828–1882). Rossetti owned a menagerie in his garden in which he kept blue peacocks from 1864 until 1871.[2] He also acquired Japanese prints and artefacts featuring peacocks when they were sold off after the South Kensington exhibition of 1862. Whistler would have been familiar both with Rossetti's

One corner of the 'Peacock Room' in Washington, DC, originally designed for a private house in London by J. M. Whistler, and decorated by him in 1876–7.

living birds and images of them in his Japanese prints. Whistler himself owned several Japanese prints, including one of a peacock that hung in his sitting room at his house in Lindsey Row, London. Peacocks were also in evidence on imported Japanese porcelain, as illustrated by Audsley in *The Keramic Art of Japan*, published in 1875.

Rossetti assisted Leyland to purchase paintings and ceramics and, through him, Leyland became a patron of Whistler in 1867. Frederick Richard Leyland, born in Liverpool in 1831, had made a fortune in the shipping business and spent largely on a collection of works of art and Chinese porcelain. When he acquired the house in Prince's Gate in 1874, he employed artists to decorate it as a backdrop for his Asian art collections. The dining room was designed and arranged by Thomas Jeckyll (1827–1881), who covered the walls in expensive leather before he became ill in 1876, and could not finish the work. Leyland commissioned Whistler to complete the decoration. This involved the ceiling, the shutters, doors, cornice, dado and walnut wainscoting. Whistler applied gold to these areas, or rather, slightly tarnished copper covered with a transparent copper-green glaze to produce a colour he called 'greengold'.

To speed the work, Whistler was invited to live in the house, whether Leyland were present or away on business. Once his work had been finished, he decided on a new detail. He painted over the leather on the walls with wave patterns in blue, which evolved into a feather pattern, with a touch of blue in the centre, resembling the eye markings of the peacock's train plumage, as well as the throat feathers. Then he painted life-sized peacocks on the shutters, working with prussian blue on the gilded ground. One of these birds has a blue peacock's crest, the other that of a green peacock. But Whistler had now over-stepped his commission and when Leyland returned unexpectedly, in October 1876, he was not pleased. Whistler asked 2,000 guineas for his work. There followed an unseemly quarrel over money and Leyland finally paid £1,000. They partially made up their differences, but Whistler went back to the house and painted a large pair of lively, angry, fighting peacocks, immortalizing their quarrel. Sporting the crest characteristic of the green peacock, the golden birds are partly imaginative, partly realistic, apart, that is, from the discordant silver discs, or coins, in the right-hand bird's plumage, with others scattered around its feet – an allusion to Leyland having paid the artist in shillings instead of golden guineas.

The room was so famous that it attracted many visitors until Leyland's death in 1892. In 1890 an American ship owner, Charles Lang Freer (1854–1919), met Whistler and they became friends. Freer frequently visited him until the artist's death on 16 July 1903. A month later, Freer bought Whistler's *La Princesse du pays de la porcelaine*, which had once hung in the Peacock Room. On 16 May 1904 Freer also purchased the whole Peacock Room for £8,400 and the following year shipped it to his house in Detroit. After his death in 1919 it came to its last resting-place, in the Freer Gallery in Washington, DC, when Freer bequeathed the Peacock Room, as part of his art collection, to the American nation.[3]

Another, though very minor, peacock association with architecture in America was neither planned nor intended by the architect. Ladies of fashion, perambulating along the main corridor of the Waldorf Astoria Hotel, on Fifth Avenue, New York, built in 1895, occasioned its being dubbed 'Peacock Alley'. Subsequently, similar corridors in other hotels also become known as Peacock Alley.

Across Europe, the Romantic movement, with its taste for picturesque imaginative styles, was fashionable. One monarch,

Robert Reid's 1890s design for a ceiling mural of 'Sight', one of the five *Senses*, for the Great Hall in the Jefferson Building at the Library of Congress, Washington, DC.

Ludwig II of Bavaria, built fairy-tale castles, indulging his love of opulence, heavy gilding, intensely bright colours and fantastic decoration. Fond of birds, his castles were homes also to live parrots, humming birds and peacocks. One of his palaces, Linderhof, was built between 1877 and 1886. At night, when bored by official paperwork, Ludwig left the ornate palace and escaped to a Moorish kiosk, a cast-iron building with a golden dome that he had purchased and erected in the garden. Inside the kiosk, the walls and arches were intricately decorated with stained glass, a profusion of Turkish rugs, a marble fountain, mother-of-pearl inlaid furniture and vases of ostrich plumes. In an alcove, lit by illuminated stained-glass windows, stood an enamelled cast metal throne in the form of three peacocks, its long divan seat covered with rich oriental silks. The throne had been designed for Ludwig by the director of the Munich State Theatre, Franz von Seitz. The Bavarian king also ordered several

A detail of
Ludwig's
Peacock Throne.

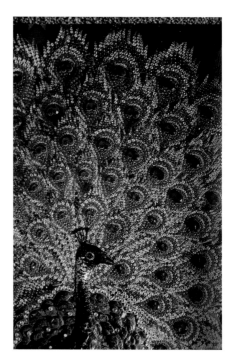

Designs by Franz
von Seitz for
Ludwig II of
Bavaria's late
19th-century
Peacock Throne,
made for Ludwig's
Moorish kiosk at
Schloss Linderhof.

craftsmen to make models of birds to decorate his apartments. The Sèvres factory made a near life-size model of a magnificent blue peacock on a plinth of flowers for him.

The technical skills required to create large ceramic models of peacocks have been mastered by very few potters. The Sèvres model was magnificently coloured and the plumage amazingly accurate, but it had a notable predecessor, created as part of a royal porcelain bird collection for the Elector Augustus the Strong. In 1717 he had bought the Japanese Palace in Dresden to accommodate his large collection of oriental and Meissen porcelain. The palace was surrounded by animal reserves and

A 1730s Meissen peacock designed by J. J. Kändler.

menageries, and when the inhabitants died, they were stuffed and transferred inside. In the royal bedroom the ornithological theme was carried through to the soft furnishings, which were made of exotic bird feathers woven together as a textile. Augustus also gave orders to the Meissen factory to model the birds in their natural sizes and colour, and many were sent to the palace between 1730 and 1740. Among them was a magnificent life-size male blue peacock that had made great demands on the master modeller Johann Gottlieb Kändler (1706–1771). He worked on the peacock for six years, after sketching it along with many other birds living in the menagerie.

In England, a life-size male blue peacock of Minton majolica glazed earthenware was close in size and style to the Sèvres and Meissen models. It was modelled by Paul Comolera in 1873. Other British factories produced much smaller peacock figures:

A full-size porcelain peacock designed by Theodor Kärner, manufactured at Nymphenberg near Munich in the 1900s.

160

around 1830, for example, the Derby porcelain factory produced a pair based on the Meissen originals, but they are stiff figures and quite small at 8.9 by 16.5 centimetres. There was also a squat Rockingham figure, a peacock displaying, 9.8 centimetres high, made between 1826 and 1842. Bow had already manufactured an unnaturally coloured peacock and a peahen about 1773. The last great full-sized porcelain peacock was made at the Nymphenberg factory near Munich about 1908, designed by Theodor Kärner. It is a magnificent example of the potter's art, unlikely to be repeated.

A modish circle of artists, based in London and including the hedonistic Oscar Wilde and his friend Whistler, turned to the east as a source of inspiration. They were reacting not only against the ugliness of industrialization but also the moralizing of the socialist Arts and Crafts Movement. Recognized now as part of an Aesthetic Movement, they promoted the idea that beauty is supreme and a philosophy of 'art for art's sake'. This echoed Ruskin's view when he had said: 'Remember that the most beautiful things in the world are the most useless, peacocks and lilies for instance.'[4] Aubrey Beardsley (1872–1898) illustrated the plays of Wilde, including the notorious *Salome* in 1894, clearly inspired by the book designs of Walter Crane and Whistler's decorations at Prince's Gate. The previous year, Beardsley's drawings for *Le Morte d'Arthur* had included a profusion of peacocks and their feathers. Whistler's Peacock Room had been the most lavish example of an Aesthetic interior. He and Wilde collected Chinese blue and white porcelain, and were influenced by a volume of sketches by the Japanese printmaker and artist Katsushika Hokusai.

Japanese wares, pottery, ivory and bronzes had been shown at the Paris Exhibition of 1862, after which the peacock became the symbol of fashionable and conspicuous opulence, the perfect motif both for the Aesthetic Movement in the 1870s and 1880s and the Art Nouveau Movement of the 1890s. The bird in Japanese art (therefore the green peacock, though the artists seem not always to have distinguished between blue and green) was to become an icon for Art Nouveau, a decorative style that spread widely over western Europe and America during the 1880s–1900s. If the Peacock Room was the outstanding example of architecture inspired by the bird, a multiplicity of artefacts created around its sinuous form and iridescent plumage by the Art Nouveau artists had a far greater and wider impact on the public consciousness.

The Japanese imports were promoted and sold in Paris and in London from the late 1870s, creating a great deal of interest and

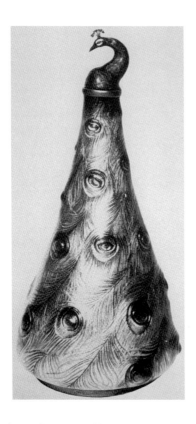

excitement, for nothing quite like them had been available for
purchase before. It was their use of curvaceous, decorative lines
and simple flat shapes that influenced the Art Nouveau artisans.
Siegfried Bing (1838–1905), a German-born French art dealer,
built up his business based on these imports and edited the peri-
odical *Le Japon artistique* from 1888. He was aware of a similar
interest in Brussels, intrigued by a new kind of art that refused to
accept the cult of the past and academic traditions. Bing adopted
this idea and named his gallery in Paris 'L'Art Nouveau'.

The French glassmaker, ceramicist and furniture designer
Emile Gallé (1846–1904) was producing pieces of glass in the
new style after taking over the family glass-making business in
Nancy in 1874. A famous French jeweller, who was trained in
Paris and London, René Lalique (1860–1945), took over the
workshop of the Parisian jeweller Jules d'Estape in 1885 and rev-
olutionized jewellery design, using vividly coloured gemstones
in motifs of flowers and nymphs. He added glass-making to his
repertoire in 1898 and his designs later came to embody Art
Nouveau motifs. Their goods were sold by Bing in Paris, but
selling Art Nouveau at its most luxurious occurred in Georges
Fouquet's Parisian shop, which was redesigned in 1895 with an

Art Nouveau interior to suggest luxury and opulence to customers from the moment they stepped over the entrance. The shop counter featured two statues of peacocks, one of them displaying – perfect examples of vanity and ostentation.

In America, Louis Comfort Tiffany (1848–1933) began working with glass in 1873 and set up a business in 1892. His was a highly individual form of Art Nouveau. His stained-glass pictorial windows were not broken up into leaded sections, but the colours and shapes flowed in a painterly manner. After collecting ancient Roman and Greek glass, he experimented to produce iridescent translucent glass, which he called 'favrile' when he succeeded in 1894. He made a series of windows designed by leading French artists in 1895, while his lamps and glassware were shown

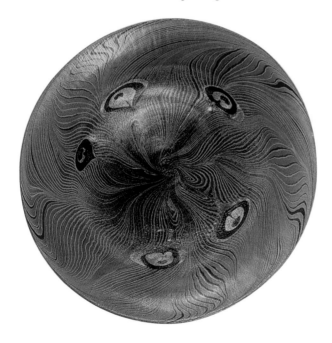

A typical favrile-glass plate with an Art Nouveau peacock pattern much used by the Tiffany studios.

at the Paris gallery of Siegfried Bing from 1898 onwards. His presence at exhibitions in Paris furthered his business success.

A poor man's, rather crude, imitation of Tiffany's glass called Carnival Ware was made by several factories in Ohio and Pennsylvania, each with their own distinctive patterns. One of the Northwood Glass Company's more famous designs, 'Peacock at the Fountain', was patented in 1914. Carnival glass was made of cheap pressed glass sprayed with solutions of metallic salts that developed into peacock colours as the glass cooled. It was popular at fairgrounds, hence its name.

The greatest output of American art pottery occurred from about 1870, with cheaper vases, cups, bowls, charges, jardinières and tiles pouring onto the market. One of the better known manufacturers, the pottery firm of Rookwood, became prominent from the early 1880s. The attempt to catch the iridescence of the peacock's plumage, its form and shape on vases and dishes, was universal to all these craftsmen, whether working in glass, with jewels or in ceramics. These goods were mostly for the American wealthy or middle-income groups.

Art Nouveau was introduced to the rest of America more by posters than by the expensive wares of Tiffany. In the 1890s there was a poster craze, fuelled by the covers on magazines: *Harpers, Century* and *Lippincott's*. Bold, dramatic designs in bright colours were perfectly tailored to the form of the peacock. Similar designs appeared on book and theatre programme covers. A rather more mundane use of peacock designs appeared on the packaging for goods as diverse as gourmet groceries and cosmetics.

The peacock feather was also employed as a motif, from Auguste Delaherche's and Rookwood's elegant vases at one extreme, to real feathers attached to printed scenic backgrounds on Edwardian postcards at the other end of the aesthetic spectrum. Peacock feathers also sweep across glass and ceramic surfaces with

delicate interplay of iridescent colour and pattern tracery. An example of art pottery currently very popular, still manufactured, and whose early pieces are sought after today, was made at the factory set up by William Moorcroft in 1913. An early Florian ware vase typifies the style that made him famous. The peacock feather was a favourite symbol used by Liberty's, who sponsored Moorcroft. Arthur Lasenby Liberty had opened a shop in Regent Street, London, in 1875, importing oriental goods and introducing London shoppers to Continental Art Nouveau.

An American Art Nouveau pottery vase of 1900 from the Rookwood Pottery with peacock feather motif by Carl Schmidt.

A Moorcroft Florian ware vase of 1902.

Peacocks helped to advertise and decorate packaging of luxury goods. Before the First World War 'Peacock' brand tea was produced in China and packed by the China Tea Company of Hong Kong.

An Edwardian Christmas card with attached peacock feathers.

In Russia, the royal family were patrons of the superb crafts-man Fabergé. One of the famous Fabergé eggs, the Peacock Egg, was made to be presented by Tsar Nicholas II to his mother in 1908. Inside the rock-crystal egg is a gold and enamelled pea-cock which can be taken out and wound up so that it struts to and fro, moving its head and displaying its train. It is said that it took the workman responsible for the mechanical model three years to complete, beginning with a life-sized model and gradually reducing it to its miniature scale. The tail feathers are in various colours of enamel. The bird may be a copy of an automaton peacock by James Cox in the Hermitage Museum.

One of the most remarkable examples of the peacock in architecture at this period was carved in ivory. Queen Victoria succumbed to the lure of the orient, especially after she had been declared Empress of India by the Disraeli administration in 1876. She revelled in this role, and had Indian servants in her households. The exotic Durbar Room at Osborne House,

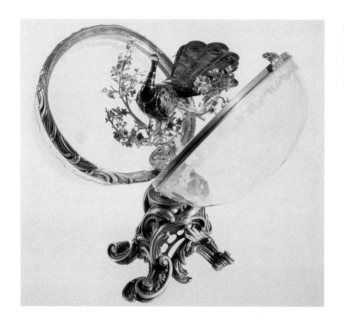

A Fabergé peacock egg by Henrik Wigström, presented by Tsar Nicholas II to his mother in 1908.

designed in 1890 by John Lockwood Kipling (father of Rudyard Kipling) with Bhai Ram Singh, echoes Indian culture and art, and housed presents from that country. Much of the room was decorated in ivory cut in intricate designs by Indian craftsmen, including a carved ivory peacock over the fireplace.

Examples of the peacock motif in pottery made by the Doulton, Minton and Wedgwood factories were sold at Liberty's. The Doulton factory was a keen employer of women decorators of their pottery. A very talented craftswoman, Florence Barlow, created a Doulton ware vase with a hand-painted peacock about 1885.[5] Doulton's Crown Lambeth was made of a very fine earthenware, again decorated by hand-painting and repeated glazing and firing to give a rich gradation of mellow tones. Also from Doulton, the dense off-white stoneware Carrara

The American television company NBC's stylized peacock logo.

vases had a translucent matt glaze similar to Carrara marble. The vases, including some with peacocks, were decorated with coloured pigments, some lustre glazes and gilding.

After 1900, Art Nouveau continued to flourish until the First World War, which put an end to the exuberant Edwardian era with its enjoyment of luxury and pleasures, beauty for its own sake and expensive toys. The peacock, a symbol of so much that is considered exotic, once again faded into the background. During the rest of the twentieth century, the live bird was to be found only in some extensive gardens where their presence was sometimes echoed in the form of topiary birds, cut into ever-green hedges. Originally, topiary birds were ornaments of gardens of grand design, first known to have been cut into Roman garden hedges. Later, they became fashionable in Britain and examples of such large-scale peacocks may be seen in the gardens of Warwick Castle, Little Moreton Hall, Hadden Hall, Great Dixter, Bedfont and Houghton Lodge, among others. Nowadays, creating topiary peacocks is no longer the preserve of the gentry, but is popular with cottage gardeners, who skil-fully snip yew, box, holly and privet into shape.

Twentieth-century literary peacocks are as scarce as their live congeners, though American Flannery O'Connor (1926–1964), who had a great liking for the bird, made several references to them in his writing, as did D. H. Lawrence. Peacock music is even rarer, but the Hungarian musician Zoltán Kodály wrote *Variations on a Hungarian Folksong (The Peacock)* in 1939, drawing on a country folksong about the Mari people's story of the flight of a peacock to the town-hall prison to free many young men incarcerated there. The mood of the music is optimistic, with a promise of a new, better future – a promise needed as much today for the peacock as humanity. Twentieth-century bird artists preferred to paint realistic pictures of birds

170

A topiary peacock clipped from a hedging honeysuckle (*Lonicera* 'Bagison's Gold') over a wire frame by Brian Joyce of Wheathampstead, Hertfordshire.

in their natural surroundings. The artist Mildred Butler made several attempts to integrate a peacock into a natural habitat scene, but whatever scenery surrounds a peacock it still looks theatrical.

Today many people travel to far-flung parts of the globe, where they may be surprised by natives still wearing peacock feathers in their hair, or to see feathers in hats as in some eastern European countries, or be able to buy peacock feather fans, as in Yunnan markets. Many will have seen peacocks wandering freely in and out of Indian temples, or strutting near visitor's centres in Indo-Chinese national parks. At home, flower arrangers may purchase peacock feathers in local florists' shops, while it is possible to see the birds, of both blue and green species, being bred by private aviculturalists or in zoos and safari parks. Just occasionally, villagers are surprised, delighted or alarmed by the arrival of a peacock in their midst.

Mikhail Larionov, *Peacocks*, 1910, oil on canvas. The peahen is a little more prominent than in many peacock paintings.

One is manageable, but when a muster of a dozen or more arrive unexpectedly and start strutting round, scratching cars, spoiling garden plants and screeching early in the morning, some residents may react adversely, although others villagers will admire the birds' great beauty and welcome them. This mixed reaction is typical of human attitudes to these wonderful birds. The newspaper report of one invasion evoked a delightful letter from a reverend gentleman who had experienced a similar invasion in his village. He had a muster of seventeen fly in and appreciated their traffic calming effect. The peacock numbers dwindled over the following weeks, which he put down to natural wastage, road accidents and a few exotic medieval banquets, until a solitary male remained. Named Percy, he

A male blue peacock 'in his pride'.

haunted the rectory garden, paraded over the front porch and accepted raisins and sultanas as an offering. He lunched daily and freely at the local pub, and 'loved nothing better than an appreciative audience' for his displays. [6]

Peacocks are guaranteed to give us as much visual pleasure today as they have given to countless thousands over past centuries. For anyone who has seen a peacock raise and fan out his glittering, shimmering train, it is an awesome sight, one that leaves an indelible memory of the 'peacock in his pride'.

Timeline of the Peacock

5.3–1.8 million BC	2600–1800 BC	c. 1500 BC	950 BC
An Ethiopian fossil from the Pleiocene era links the Asian *Pavo* peacocks with the African *Afropavo* peacock, but is more like the *Pavo* species	Indus Valley civilization makes pots decorated with peacocks	Hindu sacred books include peacocks in the stories	Solomon of Judea's ships trade with Hiram of Tyre and bring him peacocks

c. 1067–70	c. 1100–1400	14th century	15th century	16th century
Bayeux tapestry has peacocks in the border above William the Conqueror	Many illuminated manuscripts include peacocks	William Langland and Geoffrey Chaucer refer to peacocks in their poems	Peacocks widely known in Europe: in gardens, decorating men's hats and helmets, and used to fletch arrows	The pavane, a Spanish dance, becomes popular in England

1775	1804	c. 1860–90	1876–7	1886–91
Queen Marie Antoinette of France starts fashion for wearing plumes in a coiffure	Burmese green peafowl given subspecies name of *spicifer*	Peacock motif used extensively by the Arts and Crafts Movement	Whistler paints The Peacock Room in Frederick R. Leyland's London home	National Audubon Society of America and the Society for the Protection of Birds formed to prevent the exploitation of birds for their feathers

4th century BC	1st century AD	6th century AD	9th–11th century AD
Phoenician traders have taken peacocks to Greece by now	Romans importing and eating peacocks	Aesop of Samos writes down *Fables*; a Samos coin shows a displaying peacock on the prow of a boat	Peacock feather placed in a Viking grave in Oslo

1600	17th century	c. 1680	1739	1774
Aldrovandi publishes the first picture of a green peacock, sent from Japan to the pope	Mughal artists painting miniatures	Live green birds taken to Japan	The peacock throne, built in 1629, is taken from Delhi to Persia	First reported use of peacock feathers for fly-fishing

1890s–1914	1937	post 1945	1949	1963
Working in the Art Nouveau style, Lalique, Fabergé and Tiffany adopt the peacock as a symbol of luxury and beauty	Chapin describes Congo's Mbulu bird; the west first becomes aware of the Congo peacock	Nature reserves created to protect green and Congo peacocks	Indo-Chinese green peacock given subspecies name of *imperator*	Blue peacock becomes the national bird of India

References

1 NATURAL HISTORY

1 Antoine Louchart, 'A True Peafowl in Africa', *South African Journal of Science*, XCIX/7–8 (2003).

2 C. W. Beebe, *A Monograph of the Pheasants* (London, 1918–22), vol. I, *Blue Peacocks*, pp. 220–51.

3 Charles Darwin, *The Descent of Man and Selection in Relation to Sex* (London, 1871), p. 485.

4 Marion Petrie, 'Improved Growth and Survival of Offspring of the Peacocks with More Elaborate Trains', *Nature*, CCCLXXI (1994), pp. 598–9. Marion Petrie and A. Williams, 'Peahens Lay More Eggs for Peacocks with Large Trains', *Proceedings of the Royal Society of London*, Series B, XXV (1993), pp. 127–31.

5 Darwin, *The Descent of Man*, p. 454.

6 Edward Charles Stuart Baker, *The Game Birds of India, Burma and Ceylon* (London, 1921–30), vol. III, p. 84. Baker (1864–1944), sportsman and author, served in India from 1883 to 1912.

7 Thomas Williamson, *Oriental Field Sports*, 2nd edn (London, 1819), vol. II: 'About the Jungleterry District, especially near Terriagully, I have seen such quantities of pea-fowls, as absolutely surprised me! Whole woods were covered with their beautiful plumage, to which a rising sun imparted additional brilliancy . . . And I speak within bounds when I assert, that there could not be less than twelve or fifteen hundred pea-fowls, of various sizes, within sight of the spot where I stood for near an hour' (p. 61). 'The most certain mode of killing one or two birds, is by stealing under the trees at night: if there be a clear moon, so much the better' (p. 63).

8 Christopher Lever, *Naturalized Birds of the World* (New York, 1987), pp. 186–9.

9 David Taylor, *Going Wild* (London, 1980), p. 20.

10 John Latham, *Index Ornithologicus* (London, 1790–1801), vol. II, Japan peacock, p. 672, and the white peacock, p. 617. The black-winged blue peacock was first mentioned by John Latham in *A General History of Birds* (London, 1823), vol. VIII, p. 114.

11 Jean Delacour, 'A New Species of *Pavo muticus*', *The Ibis*, XCI (1949), pp. 348–9. 'In *The Ibis*, 31 (1928) I have pointed out for the first time the considerable difference existing between the western Burmese and the Malaysian-Indochinese forms of the Green Peafowl. I now find that the population inhabiting French Indochina, western Burma and Siam south to the Isthmus of Kra can be separated from those of Malaya . . . For the Indochinese population I propose the name Pavo Muticus imperator.'

12 *Pavo muticus spicifer*, Shaw and Nodder, 1804, was called 'Spiked Peacock' in the text of vol. XVI, pl. 641 of the *Naturalist's Miscellany*. 'Spica' is Latin for an ear of corn, which well describes the shape of the green peacock's crest. Aldrovandus had depicted a female green peacock with a stem and ear of wheat alongside.

13 Baker, *The Game Birds of India, Burma and Ceylon*, p. 85.

14 Herbert Wendt, *Out of Noah's Ark* (London, 1956), pp. 427–34.

15 D. Jeggo, *Peafowl, Afropavo congensis*, 9th Annual Report, Jersey Wildlife Preservation Trust (1972), pp. 43–9.

16 Walter Verheyen, 'The Congo Peacock at Antwerp Zoo', *International Zoo Yearbook* (London), IV (1962), pp. 87–91, and V (1963), pp. 127–8.

2 UNNATURAL HISTORY

1 Steven Lonsdale, *Animals and the Origins of Dance* (London, 1981), pp. 81–2.

2 Angelo de Gubernatis, *Zoological Mythology* (London, 1872), vol. II, pp. 326–7.

3 T. P. Gardiner, *Peafowl: Their Conservation, Breeding and*

Management (Reading, 1996), p. 1.

4 St Augustine, *De civitate dei / The City of God* (New York, 1950), bk 21, ch. 4, p. 766.

5 Peter Bull, in the *Observer Supplement* (24 November 1968). The play 'Cage me a Peacock' was by Noel Langley (London, 1935).

6 Iona Opie and Moira Tatem, *A Dictionary of Superstitions* (Oxford, 1989), p. 301.

7 J. Stephenson, *The Zoological Section of the Nuzhatu-l-Qulub, by Hamdullah Al-Mostaufi Al-Qazwini*, ed. and trans. J. Stephenson (London, 1928).

8 C. W. Beebe, *A Monograph of the Pheasants* (London, 1918–22), vol. III, p. 244.

3 THE BLUE INDIAN PEACOCK AT HOME

1 Mortimer Wheeler, *Civilization of the Indus Valley and Beyond* (London, 1966), p. 52; Time Life, *Ancient India, Land of Mystery* (London, 2005), pp. 9–36.

2 Time Life, *Ancient India*, pp. 27–30.

3 Claudius Aelian, *On the Characteristics of Animals, with an English Translation by A. F. Schofield* (Cambridge, MA, and London, 1958),book VIII, 18 and book XIII, 18.

4 Lesley Adkins, *Empires of the Plain: Henry Rawlinson and the Lost Languages of Babylon* (London, 2003), p. 40.

5 Reginald Heber also wrote *Narrative of a Journey through India, 1828* and penned the hymns 'From Greenland's icy mountains, From India's coral strand . . . What though the spicy breezes Blow soft o'er Ceylon's isle' (1827).

6 William Bernhard Tegetmeier, *The Poultry Book*: *Comprising the Breeding and Management of Profitable and Ornamental Poultry*, 2nd edn (London, 1873), p. 327.

7 A. O. Hume and C.M.T. Marshall, *The Game Birds of India, Burmah and Ceylon* (Calcutta, 1879–81; London, 1913–17), p. 83–4. Allan Octavian Hume worked in the Indian Civil Service from 1848 to 1882 and was a big-game hunter, ornithologist and

botanist, amassing the largest collection of Indian birds ever known. He bequeathed his collection to the British Museum (Natural History), now the Natural History Museum, London.

8 Conference of the International Council for Bird Preservation, Tokyo, 1960. Reported in the Council's *Annual Report for 1960*, British Section, Resolution 9, p. 14. (The robin was chosen as Britain's national bird.)

9 Time Life, *Ancient India*, pp. 109–10.

10 Some maintain that Galle might be the Tarshish supplying King Solomon with his 'ivory, apes and peacocks'. They cite evidence that these products were known to the old Hebrew writers by the same names as they now bear among the Tamils of Sri Lanka. Ernst Haeckel, *Indische Reisebriefe* (Berlin, 1883), ch. 9.

11 Sir James E. Tennent, *Ceylon: An Account of the Island, Physical, Historical and Topographical*, 5th edn (London, 1860), vol. I, part 2, Zoology, ch. II, 'Birds', pp. 164–5.

12 'Peacock in the Poison Grove' by the Tibetan author Dharmarakshita, edited from the *Shariputra Sutra*, trans. William Woodville Rockhill (London, 1897).

13 Tennent, *Ceylon*, ch. III.

4 THE BLUE INDIAN PEACOCK GOES WEST

1 There is no evidence that peacocks were introduced into Egypt at this time, despite several writers asserting that they were. A careful search by the author through countless texts and illustrations of Egyptian tombs and other buildings provided only negative results. This lack of evidence was confirmed by Patrick F. Houlihan, in *The Birds of Ancient Egypt* (Cairo, 1988), which did not include the peacock, and his article in *Ancient Egypt Magazine*, IV/3 (December 2003–January 2004). The earliest evidence is found in Ptolemaic Egypt. Antero Tammisto, *Birds in Mosaics* (Rome, 1994), p. 270, confirms this. Ptolemy I (323–283 BC); Ptolemy II (285–246 BC, at first ruling jointly with his father).

2 Bible, II Chronicles 8.18, 9.21; I Kings 22.48.

3 Several birds wrongly have the adjective *guinea*, *guinienis*, i.e. from Guinea, in their names, given to them by scientists receiving skins from ships returning from Guinea, West Africa. They were, however, Asian species that had been carried to Guinea and transferred onto European ships trading only as far as ports on the coast of Guinea. Similarly, the Tarshish ships trading south to Ophir would collect the peacocks, originally from the Indus Valley, on their return journey from the East African coast, while calling in at South Yemen ports.

4 David Rohl, *The Lost Testament, from Eden to Exile: the Five-Thousand Year History of the People of the Bible* (London, 2002), pp. 371–5.

5 Bible, I Kings 22: 48; Job 39: 13.

6 Frederick E. Zeuner, *A History of Domesticated Animals* (London, 1963), p. 456. No references are given for this statement.

7 Darius III ascended the 'Peacock Throne' in Babylon in 336 BC.

8 T. P. Gardiner, *Peafowl: Their Conservation, Breeding and Management* (Reading, 1996), p. 2.

9 George Jennison, *Animals for Show and Pleasure in Ancient Rome* (Manchester, 1937), p. 16. Antiphanes wrote some time between 400 and 336 BC.

10 Aristophanes, *Birds* (414 BC), 11. 102. 269.

11 Victor Hehn, *The Wanderings of Plants and Animals from their First Home* (London, 1885), pp. 264–6.

12 Gerald Durrell, *Beasts in my Bed* (Glasgow, 1973), p. 185.

13 Aristotle, *The Works of Aristotle Translated into English*, vol. IV: *Historia animalium* (Oxford, 1910), book VI, 564b.

14 J.R.S. Phillips, *The Medieval Expansion of Europe* (Oxford, 1998), p. 3.

15 Oliver Goldsmith, *A History of the Earth and Animated Nature* (London and Edinburgh, 1774), book IV, p. 60, quoted Pliny Secundus (AD 23–70).

16 Jennison, *Animals for Show and Pleasure in Ancient Rome*, p. 109.

17 Marcus Valerius Martial, *Epigrams*, XXX, 70.

18 Hehn, *Wanderings of Plants and Animals*, p. 268. Lucian (*c*. AD 115–200) was a writer of satirical dialogues in Athens.

19 Claudius Aelian, *On the Characters of Animals* (Cambridge, MA, 1958), book V, 21, pp. 313–15.

20 Henry Sweet, *The Oldest English Texts* (London, 1885), p. 85, no. 1505, pavo: pauua; p. 588, pawa, peacock.

21 Brunsdon Yapp, *Birds in Medieval Manuscripts* (New York and London, 1981), p. 20. The Gospel book is in Trinity College, Cambridge, MS.B.10.4 (James 215), f. 9r.

22 Francis Klingender, *Animals in Art and Thought to the End of the Middle Ages* (London, 1871; new edn 1971), p. 390.

23 *Fairbairn's Book of Crests* (Edinburgh, 1902), vol. I, p. 435.

24 The ultimate source of this comparison, via Porphyry, Plato, Socrates, Solomon and Aristotle, is *Physiologus*, a text once attributed to Epiphanius.

25 Geoffrey Chaucer, *Complete Works* (London, 1912, reprint 1969), Reeve's Tale, line 6; Prologue, line 104; Parlement of Foules, line 356.

26 G. L. Remnant, *A Catalogue of Misericords in Great Britain* (London, 1969).

27 Details of this feast are in British Library, Harley MS 4016. Quoted in Peter Brears et al., *A Taste of History: 10,000 Years of Food in Britain* (London, 1993), p. 125.

28 Frederick J. Furnivall, ed., *Early English Meals and Manners* (London, 1868), p. 103, quoting John Russell's *Book of Nurture*.

29 Bryant Lillywhite, *London Signs* (London, 1972), pp. 402–4.

30 Ibid., p. 403.

31 Sarah Boehme and Emma I. Hansen, 'The feathered cape and painted proof: Stearns painting resolves mystery on origin of unusual feathered capes', *Points West* (Spring 1997).

32 *The Auk*, V (1988), pp. 334–5.

33 C. W. Beebe, *A Monograph of the Pheasants* (London, 1918–22), vol. III, p. 251.

5 THE GREEN PEACOCK IN THE EAST

1 C. W. Beebe, *A Monograph of the Pheasants* (London, 1918–22), vol. III, p. 260; vol. III, pp. 220–51, Indian blue peacock; pp. 251–63,

green peacock.

2 Ibid., vol. III, p. 260.
3 Jean Delacour, *Pheasants of the World* (London, 1951), p. 366.
4 Keith Howman, *Pheasants of the World: Their Breeding and Management* (Surrey, BC, 1993), p. 170, and T. P. Gardiner, *Peafowl: Their Conservation, Breeding and Management* (Reading, 1996), p. 24.
5 William Warren, *Arts and Crafts of Thailand* (London, 2001), p. 125.
6 Gardiner, *Peafowl*, p. 23.
7 C. Scott Lyttleton, ed., *Mythology: The Illustrated Anthology of World Myth and Storytelling* (London, 2002), p. 422.
8 Cherry Denman, *The Little Peacock's Gift: Folktales of the World* (London, 1987), is based on the Chinese Spring Festival celebrated throughout China with parties and feasting and firework displays, beautifully told and illustrated in this small book.
9 Anthony Christie, *Chinese Mythology* (London, 1968), pp. 134–5.
10 Beebe, *A Monograph of the Pheasants*, vol. III, p. 245. Beebe adds, 'In Russia, on the other hand, the peacock feather is often a part of the headdress of a servant or peasant.'
11 John Latham, *A General Synopsis of Birds* (London, 1781–5), Japan peacock, vol. IV, p. 672, as *spicifer*.
12 Conraad Jacob Temminck, *Histoire naturelle générale des pigeons et des gallinacés* (Amsterdam and Paris, 1813–15), vol. II, pp. 56–9.
13 George Ashdown Audsley, *Ornamental Art of Japan* (London, 1882)
14 Ibid.

6 ARTEFACTS AND ARCHITECTURE

1 John Ruskin, 22 October 1875, quoted in Maureen Lambourne, *The Art of Bird Illustration* (London, 1990), p. 163.
2 Gale Pedrick, *Life with Rossetti; or, No Peacocks Allowed* (London, 1964), pp. 85–6. The cries of Rossetti's birds caused strained relations with his neighbours, resulting in complaints in 1871 to the landlord, Lord Cadogan, who insisted on Rossetti's getting rid of them. Lord Cadogan also inserted clauses in subsequent leases forbidding peacocks to be kept in the gardens of his tenants.

3 Linda Merrill, *The Peacock Room: A Cultural Biography* (New Haven and London, 1998).

4 John Ruskin, *Stones of Venice* (London, 1851–3), ch. 2.

5 Florence E. Barlow joined the Lambeth Pottery in 1873. She and her sister Hannah painted quadrupeds and birds until about 1878 when they came to an agreement that only Florence would paint the birds: Desmond Eyles, *The Doulton Lambeth Wares* (London, 2002), pp. 72–4.

6 Letter from Revd D. G. Thomas, *Daily Telegraph* (8 May 2004). A muster of peacocks arrived in Cookley, Worcestershire, reported in the *Daily Telegraph* (6 May 2004). Another peacock invasion of a village, Souldrop in Bedfordshire, was reported in the *Daily Telegraph* (3 September 2005).

Bibliography

Baker, Edward Charles Stuart, *The Game Birds of India, Burma and Ceylon*, 3 vols (London, 1921–30)

Barron, John Penrose, *The Silver Coins of Samos* (London, 1966)

Beebe, William, *A Monograph of the Pheasants*, 4 vols (London, 1918–22)

Belon, Pierre, *L'Histoire de la nature des oyseaux* (Paris, 1555)

——, *Pourtraicts d'oyseaux . . .* (Paris, 1557)

Bergmann, Josef, *The Peafowl of the World* (Hindhead, Surrey, 1980)

Boudet, Jacques, *Man and Beast: A Visual History* (London, 1964)

Brewer's Dictionary of Phrase and Fable, revised by Ivor H. Evans (London, 1981)

Buffon, Georges Louis-Leclerc, Comte de, *Histoire naturelles des oiseaux*, 10 vols (Paris, 1770–86)

Clutton-Brock, Juliet, *Natural History of Domesticated Animals* (Cambridge, MA and London, 1987)

Dallapiccola, Anna L., *Dictionary of Hindu Lore and Legend* (London, 2002)

Daniel, Howard, *Encyclopaedia of Themes and Subjects in Painting* (London, 1971)

Delacour, Jean, *The Pheasants of the World*, 2nd edn (Bures, Suffolk, 1977)

Denman, Cherry, *The Little Peacock's Gift: Folktales of the World* (London, 1987)

Doughty, Robin Whitaker, *Feather Fashions and Bird Preservation: A Study in Nature Protection* (Berkeley, CA, 1975)

Elliot, Daniel Giraud, *A Monograph of the Phasianidae, or Family of Pheasants*, 2 vols (New York, 1870–72)

Fraser-Lu, Sylvia, *Burmese Crafts: Past and Present* (Oxford, 1994)

Gardiner, T. P. *Peafowl: Their Conservation, Breeding and Management* (Reading, 1996)

Gesner, Conrad, *Historiae animalium* (Zurich, 1551–8)

Gubernatis, Angelo de, *Zoological Mythology or Legends of Animals*, 2 vols (London, 1872)

Hadfield, Anna, *A Peacock on the Lawn* (London, 1965)

Hall, James, *Hall's Illustrated Dictionary of Symbols in Eastern and Western Art* (London, 1994)

Howman, K., *Pheasants of the World: Their Breeding and Management* (Surrey, BC, 1993)

Hume, Allan Octavio, and C.M.T. Marshall, *The Game Birds of India, Burmah and Ceylon*, 3 vols (London, 1913–17)

Johnsgard, Paul A., *The Pheasants of the World* (Oxford, 1986)

Kay, Charles de, *Bird Gods* (London, 1898)

Klingender, Francis, *Animals in Art and Thought to the End of the Middle Ages* (London, 1871; new edn 1971)

Lillywhite, Bryant, *London Signs* (London, 1972)

McFarlane, K. B., *Hans Memling* (London, 1971)

Mattingley, Harold, *Coins of the Roman Empire in the British Museum*, 2 vols (London, 1976)

Merrill, Linda, *The Peacock Room: A Cultural Biography* (New Haven and London, 1998)

Newton, Alfred, *A Dictionary of Birds* (London, 1896)

Pickering, David, *Cassell's Dictionary of Superstitions* (London, 1995)

Pliny, *Natural History; English translation by H. Rackham*, 10 vols (London, 1938–62)

Polo, Marco *The Book of Ser Marco Polo . . .* , ed. Sir Henry Yule, 2 vols (London, 1903)

Radford, E., and M. A. Radford, *Encyclopaedia of Superstitions*, ed. Christina Hole (London, 1962)

Reimbold, Ernst Thomas, *Der Pfau: Mythologie und Symbolik* (Munich, 1983)

Remnant, G. L., *A Catalogue of Misericords in Great Britain* (London, 1969)

Rice, E. E., *The Grand Procession of Ptolemy Philadelphus* (Oxford, 1983)

Roberts, Michael, *Peacocks Past and Present* (Cheltenham, 2003)

Rowland, Beryl, *Birds with Human Souls* (Knoxville, TN, 1978)

Shaw, George, and P. F. Nodder, *Vivarium Naturae; or, the Naturalist's Miscellany*, 24 vols (London, 1790–1813), vol. XVI

Storm, Rachel, *Indian Mythology: Myths and Legends of India, Tibet and Sri Lanka* (London, 2000)

Stratton, Carol, *Art of Sukhothai Thailand's Golden Age, mid-13thc–mid-15thc* (London, 1987)

Stromberg, L., *Peafowl Breeding and Management* (Minnesota, 1985)

Tammisto, Antero, *Birds in Mosaics: A Study on the Representations of Birds in Hellenistic and Roman-Campanian Tesselated Mosaics to the Early Augustan Age* (Rome, 1994).

Thayer, Gerald Handerson, *Concealing Coloration in the Animal Kingdom* (New York, 1909)

Wayre, Philip, *A Guide to the Pheasants of the World* (London, 1969)

Welch, Stuart Cory, *Imperial Mughal Painting* (London, 1978)

Wood, J. G., *The Illustrated Natural History* (London, 1853)

Yapp, Brunsdon, *Birds in Medieval Manuscripts* (New York and London, 1981)

Zeuner, Frederick E., *A History of Domesticated Animals* (London, 1963)

Associations and Websites

BIRD LIFE INTERNATIONAL
www.birdlife.net

THE CONGO PEAFOWL TRUST
www.nagonline.net

PEACOCK INFORMATION CENTER
www.peafowl.com

SPECIES SURVIVAL COMMISSION
OF IUCN
(the World Conservation Union)
www.iucn.org

UNITED PEAFOWL ASSOCIATION
www.peafowl.org

THE WILDLIFE CONSERVATION
SOCIETY
www.wcs.org

WORLD PHEASANT ASSOCIATION
www.pheasant.org.uk

Acknowledgements

The year 2005 in our household became the Year of the Peacock, so I am most grateful to my husband, Andrew, for his patience, interest and especially his perseverance while photographing recalcitrant blue, green and Congo peacocks during that year.

Friends who alerted me to the presence of peacocks in all materials, shapes and sizes, and for being concerned in the progress of the book, are warmly appreciated. I thank Carole Burrows, Richard Busby, Errol Fuller, W. G. Hale, Laurence Jones, Maureen Lambourne, Amberley Moore and Howard Radclyffe, for their interest and suggestions. Brian Joyce showed me his expert peacock topiary. Blue peacock owners Mary and Ken Audemard were most generous with their time while we tried to get their birds to accept us and pose unconcernedly. To be able to stand so close to displaying peacocks was a privilege, and the chicks were pure delight. Quinton Spratt allowed us to see his exquisitely beautiful, though feisty, green peacocks, who impressed us far more than we did them.

Very few people in the world have succeeded in breeding and rearing Congo peacocks. Wayne McLeod of Chester Zoo has reared them more than once and I thank him for generously sharing his enthusiasm for, and knowledge of, these extremely rare birds.

Librarians helped me search for two-dimensional peacocks, cheerfully fetching and carrying hundreds of books. I particularly thank Gina Douglas at the Linnean Society, London, Ian Dawson at the RSPB, and the librarians at Cambridge University Library and the Haverhill Public Library.

Photo Acknowledgements

The author and publishers wish to express their thanks to the below sources of illustrative material and/or permission to reproduce it. Some locations uncredited in the captions for reasons of brevity are also given below.

From U. Aldrovandus, *Ornithologia*. . . (Bologna, 1600): p. 141; from F. Barlow, *Birds and Fowles* (London, 1665): p. 116; from J. Bayer, *Uranometria*. . . (Augsburg, 1603): p. 40; from T. Bewick, *History of British Birds* (Newcastle upon Tyne, 1826): p. 16; from T. Bewick, *Select Fables* (Newcastle upon Tyne, 1820): pp. 50, 60; Bibliothèque Mazarine, Paris (Bib. Mazarine, MS 473, fol. 85*v*): p. 42; The Bodleian Library, Oxford (MS Elliot 254, f. 9r): p. 69; British Library, London (Department of Oriental Antiquities, OA 1973.9-17.03, the 'Manley *Ragamala*'): p. 62; from W. Crane, *Triplets* (London, 1899): p. 51 (foot); from D. G. Elliot, *Monograph of the Phasianidae*. . . (New York, 1871–72): p. 31; The Fogg Art Museum, Cambridge, Mass.: p. 71; Conrad Gesner, *Historiae Animalium liber III qui est de avium natura* (Zürich, 1555): p. 112; J. Gould, *Birds of Asia* (London, 1850–83): p. 39; from J. J. Grandville, *Les Animaux* (Paris, 1866): p. 9 (left); Hinohara Collection, Tokyo: p. 144; photos Andrew B. Jackson: pp. 6, 7, 17, 19, 24, 28 (foot), 30, 103, 105, 113, 129; photo courtesy of Brian Joyce: p. 171; Kedleston Hall, Derbyshire: p. 80; Kunsthistorisches Museum, Vienna: p. 114; photos Michael R. Leaman/Reaktion Books: p. 74; photos Library of Congress, Washington, DC: pp. 29 (Prints and Photographs Division, LC-USZC4-2991), 157 (LC-USZ62-93934); Musée de la Tapisserie de Bayeux: p. 97; Musée du Louvre, Paris: pp. 54, 121; Muzeum Narodowe, Gdansk: p. 109 (formerly in the Marienkirche, Danzig); National Museum of India, Delhi: p. 46; from J. Nott, *The Cook's and Confectionar's Dictionary* (London, 1723): p. 118; Palace Museum, Taipei: pp. 132, 133; private collections: pp. 13, 14, 26, 28 (top), 38, 66, 70, 150, 151; from J. Ray and F. Willughby, *Ornithologia Libri Tres* (London, 1676): p. 115; photo Rex Features/The Travel Library: p. 173 (430333A); Ruskin Gallery, Sheffield (Collection of the Guild of St George): p. 94; Schloss Adolphseck bei Fulda: p. 11 (right); Smithsonian American Art Museum, Washington, DC: p. 20; Smithsonian Institution, Washington, DC: p. 154; State Tretyakov Gallery, Moscow: p. 172; Stibbert Museum, Florence: p. 143; Topkapi Museum, Istanbul (MS Hazine 1222, a 16th-century Turkish version of the *Siyar-I-Nahi*): p. 47; photos courtesy of Rafael Valls, Duke Street, London: pp. 51 (top), 117.

Index

191